LEARNING CHINESE WHILE TRAVELING CHINA

学汉语 游中国

◎ 作者 耿京茹 夫 伯

◎ 改编 曲 径

◎ 翻译 李迎春 崔 红

王宝元 芦林平

华语教学出版社
SINOLINGUA

First Edition 2005

ISBN 7-80052-926-6

Published by Sinolingua
24 Baiwanzhuang Road, Beijing 100037, China
Tel: (86) 10-68995871
Fax: (86) 10-68326333
Site : www.sinolingua.com.cn
E-mail:hyjx@ sinolingua.com.cn
Printed by Beijing Songyuan Printing Co. Ltd.
Distributed by China International
Book Trading Corporation
35 Chegongzhuang Xilu, P.O. Box 399
Beijing 100044, China

Printed in the People's Republic of China

Learning Chinese While Traveling in China is compiled for those who are eager to visit China, but can't speak good Chinese or can't speak it at all. It is compiled in Chinese with English translation and Chinesc phonetic symbols suited to the needs of beginners. It is a practical textbook for travelers, containing dialogues which you will find useful in many situations. Furthermore, it is more practical and useful for tourists by progressing through different stages of study: first basic dialogues, then dialogues specifically designed for tourists.

In addition, *Learning Chinese While Traveling in China* is rich in tourist information as well as tourist guidelines to specific areas. It provides necessary and relevant information for tourists, both in the scenic spots and historic sites in Beijing, Shanghai, Chongqing, Xi'an and other places that you are bound to visit in China, and in shopping malls, hotels, restaurants and other places.

We hope *Learning Chinese While Traveling in China* will be a great help and a good friend to you.

Please take *Learning Chinese While Traveling in China* with you on your trip to China, and may you have a wonderful trip.

Compilers

Quick Index of Expressions

Part One Basic Dialogues

Part Two Dialogues for Touring

On the Airplane

Entering a Country

Sightseeing

Recreation and Entertainment

Telephone / Post Office / Bank

Accidents

Illness

Returning to Your Home Country

Part Three Travel Information

Part Four Famous Tourist Sites in China

Appendix

Quick Index of Expressions

Greetings

Self-introduction

Thanks and Apologies

- Thanks a lot. **1**
- My sincere thanks. **2**
- Thank you. **3**
- Thank you for all your help. **4**
- Don't mention it. **5**
- It's my pleasure. **6**
- I apologize. **7**
- I'm very sorry. **8**
- I've been a lot of trouble to you. **9**
- It's all right /no big deal. **10**

Uncertainty

- Sorry. Would you please say that again? **1**
- Sorry. I don't understand. **2**
- I only speak a little Chinese. **3**
- Does anyone here speak English (French)? **4**
- How do you say this in English? **5**
- What's this? **6**
- Who is he (she)? **7**
- Where is it? **8**
- Which one is it? **9**
- What time? **10**

Affirmative/Negative Expressions

- Yes. 1
- No. 2
- Fine. 3
- It's all right. 4
- Got it. 5
- I see. 6
- OK. It is settled. 7
- Not necessary now. 8
- I am sorry. I cannot be of help to you. 9
- Is it OK? 10

Numbers and Expressions(I)

- Eleven, twelve, thirteen 1
- Fourteen, fifteen, sixteen 2
- Seventeen, eighteen, nineteen 3
- Twenty, thirty, forty 4
- Fifty, sixty, seventy 5
- Eighty, ninety, one hundred 6
- One thousand, ten thousand, one hundred thousand 7
- One million, ten million, one hundred million 8
- Six thousand three hundred and forty, six thousand eight hundred and ninety 9
- Three thousand six hundred and seventy-two, sixteen thousand three hundred and forty-three 10

Numbers and Expressions (Ⅱ)

- One person, two people, three people, a few people 1
- One, two, three, a few 2
- One set of, two sets of, three sets of, several sets of 3
- One basket of, two baskets of, three baskets of, a few baskets of 4
- One bottle of, two bottles of, three bottles of, a few bottles of 5
- One cup of, two cups of, three cups of, a few cups of 6
- Room one, Room two, Room three, Room XXX 7
- One copy of, two copies of, three copies of, a few copies of 8
- One, two, three, a few 9
- One piece of, two pieces of, three pieces of, a few pieces of 10

Time and Expressions

- What hour, two o'clock, six o'clock, 12 o'clock 1
- A few minutes, five minutes, fifteen minutes, twenty-five minutes 2
- Thirty minutes, forty minutes, forty-five minutes, fifty minutes 3
- Which month, January, February, March 4
- September, October, November, December 5
- What date, the 1st, the 4th, the 10th 6
- What day, Monday, Tuesday, Wednesday 7
- Thursday, Friday, Saturday, Sunday 8
- Two days, three days, five days, six days 9
- Several weeks, one week, two weeks 10

Looking for Seats

· Good afternoon! 1

· Please show me your boarding pass. 2

· OK. Here is my boarding pass. 3

· It's 35D. 4

· Where is this seat? 5

· Please walk ahead to the right (left). 6

· I am sorry. Please make way for me. 7

· Airhostess, the lid of the luggage trunk won't shut. 8

· Excuse me, I think that 35D is my seat. 9

· Would it be too much trouble for you to switch seats with him (her)? 10

Accepting Service

· Coffee or black tea? 1

· I would like coffee (black tea). 2

· What would you care to drink? 3

· I would like a beer (juice). 4

· One more cup of beer, please. 5

· A cup of water for me, please. 6

· Can I have a piece of customs declaration form? 7

· Do you have French newspapers (magazines)? 8

· I would like to buy some wine and perfume. 9

· May I turn the air off? 10

Airsickness or Related Situations

- My stomach is upset. **1**
- I am going to throw up. **2**
- Do you have any medicine for airsickness (headaches)? **3**
- Please let me have a pillow and a blanket. **4**
- Please give me an airsickness bag. **5**
- Is there a doctor here? **6**
- Is there a hostess here who speaks French? **7**
- Where is the toilet? **8**
- What is this medicine for? **9**
- I feel much better, thanks. **10**

Arrival

- Where are we flying to now? **1**
- Will we arrive on time? **2**
- What time do we get to Beijing? **3**
- What's the weather like in Beijing? **4**
- Is there any delay? **5**
- How long will the delay be? **6**
- Can I go to the toilet now? **7**
- Can I get up from the seat now? **8**
- Can I take out my luggage now? **9**
- It has been a tiring journey. **10**

Entry Check

- How long do you plan to stay in China? **1**
- I will stay for one week. **2**
- What's your purpose of travel? **3**
- For pleasure (to attend business meetings). **4**
- What's your occupation? **5**
- I work in a trade company. **6**
- I am a student (housewife). **7**
- Where do you plan to stay? **8**
- In Beijing Hotel. **9**
- I haven't decided yet. **10**

Luggage Retrieval

- Where do I get my luggage from flight 702 on US Northwest? **1**
- Please help me find my luggage. **2**
- My luggage is not yet found. **3**
- How many pieces of luggage do you have? **4**
- Two—a leather suitcase and a handbag. **5**
- Here is my luggage custody card. **6**
- Please fill in this form. **7**
- I've filled it in. **8**
- Once we find your luggage, where should we send it? **9**
- Please contact me at this place/number. **10**

Customs Inspections

- Do you have anything to declare? **1**
- I don't have anything to declare. **2**
- There is a pack of cigarettes and two bottles of wine. **3**
- What's in this bag? **4**
- Some gifts and articles of daily use. **5**
- Please open the leather case. **6**
- What's this? **7**
- It is a gift for a friend, a pen. **8**
- This watch and diamond are for my own use. **9**
- I bought them a year (two years/three years) ago. **10**

Changing Money and Taking a Bus

- Where is the bank? **1**
- I want to change money. **2**
- I would like to cash my traveler's check for RMB. **3**
- Please give me 10 100-yuan RMB notes. **4**
- Please change these two hundred RMB notes to coins. **5**
- Where do I catch the shuttle bus? **6**
- Could I trouble you to go with me? **7**
- I'd like to buy a ticket to Qianmen (Xidan). **8**
- May I ask how much the fare is to Dongdan? **9**
- How much is a ticket to Zhongguancun? **10**

Taking a Taxi

- May I ask where the taxi station is? **1**
- Could you get a taxi for me? **2**
- About how much is it to the Beijing Railway Station? **3**
- Please take me to the Beijing Railway Station. **4**
- Please take me to this address. **5**
- Please stop at the traffic lights. **6**
- Stop here. **7**
- Excuse me. Can we make a stop here? **8**
- Here is a one-hundred RMB note. Do you have enough change? **9**
- Please wait for me a little bit here. **10**

Taking Subways/Railways

- Where is the nearest subway station? **1**
- Where do I get off to change to the loop line? **2**
- How much is it roughly to Qianmen station? **3**
- Where do I get off to catch a bus to Qianmen station? **4**
- What's the next stop? **5**
- Is the next stop Qianmen station? **6**
- How many stations do we pass before I get off? **7**
- Could I trouble you to tell me when we get to Qianmen station? **8**
- Please sell me two return tickets to Xi'an. **9**
- Please sell me three adult tickets and one child ticket to Xi'an. **10**

Taking Buses

Renting a Car

- I would like to rent a car. **1**
- Here is my international driver's license. **2**
- Show me your price listings. **3**
- Do you have a car catalogue? **4**
- Do you have a 2,000-ml. auto car? **5**
- I would like to have this one. **6**
- Do you want insurance? **7**
- Is gasoline included? **8**
- What's the best way to contact you in case of an accident? **9**
- Do you have a foreign language (French) driving map? **10**

Reserving a Room

- Where is the travel agency? **1**
- Can I book a room in the Beijing Hotel here? **2**
- Please help me find a clean and inexpensive hotel. **3**
- I would like something near the Beijing Railway Station (Airport) area **4**
- How many minutes does it take on foot from the Beijing Railway Station? **5**
- I would like a room for less than 500 RMB per day. **6**
- I would like to book a room in the Youth Hostel. **7**
- Please refer me to some other hotels. **8**
- Is there a more economical hotel (room)? **9**
- How much is it per person each day? **10**

Check-in/Check-out

- My name is Mike. My room is booked in advance in New York. 1
- It was booked at the airport (travel agency). 2
- I want a single (double) room. 3
- Is service fee (tax) included? 4
- Does the room rate include breakfast? 5
- Is a reservation required for breakfast? 6
- Please leave these valuables at the service desk. 7
- Please take my luggage to my room. 8
- I would like a very quiet room. 9
- Excuse me , please let me have a room with a view. 10
- Can I take a look at the room? 11
- I would like to check out now. 12
- When is the latest check-out time? 13
- I would like to stay for one more day. 14
- I would like to check out one day earlier. Is that all right with you? 15
- Do you take traveler's checks (credit cards)? 16
- I want to leave my valuables with you. 17
- Could you call the porter for me? 18
- Would you get a taxi for me? 19
- Where is the shuttle bus? 20

Complaint

- Excuse me. I am not satisfied with this room. May I change to another room? 1
- The room key is broken. 2
- I left my key in my room. 3
- Maybe the air conditioning (heat) has broken down. 4
- Please adjust the air to make this room warmer. 5
- There is no hot water in the bathroom. 6
- There is no towel (soap). 7
- The light in the room (bathroom) is broken. 8
- The TV (reading lamp) won't work. 9
- There is no tap water in the lavatory (The tap water in the lavatory runs nonstop). 10

Asking for Services

- Please send me two sandwiches and two cups of tomato juice. 1
- I'm in room 505, and I would like some ice and water. 2
- I would like to have breakfast in my room. 3
- When does the coffee shop open (close)? 4
- Please wake me up at six o'clock tomorrow morning. 5
- Are there any messages for me? 6
- Pardon me. Please send me one more quilt (bath towel). 7
- Do you provide fax services? 8
- Please have this jacket dry cleaned (ironed). 9
- Please clean up the room. 10

Looking for Restaurants

- Is there any place nearby where we can eat? **1**
- Is there a restaurant which serves Western food near here? **2**
- Are there any restaurants with a local flavor in this area? **3**
- Are there any hotels that offer reasonably priced food near here? **4**
- Do you know of any inexpensive eateries around here? **5**
- Any other restaurants? **6**
- I would like to book a table for 7 p.m. today (tomorrow). **7**
- Is a suit mandatory? **8**
- I would like to book a private room. **9**
- Please let me have a seat by the window. **10**

At the Gate of a Restaurant

- My name is Martin, and I have booked a table for 7:30. **1**
- Welcome. Do you have a reservation? **2**
- Yes. **3**
- No. Are there any tables available? **4**
- How many of you are there? **5**
- There are four of us. **6**
- Please wait a moment. **7**
- How long will we have to wait? **8**
- How do you like these seats? **9**
- Fine. They are OK. Thanks. **10**

Ordering a Meal and Other Requests

- What would you like to order? 1
- Please show me your menu. 2
- What dish is this? 3
- Tell us about your chef's specialties today. 4
- What dish can be made the fastest? 5
- What dishes are not cooked with pork (chicken/beef)? 6
- I would like a vegetable (cream) soup. 7
- Please grill mine rare (well-done). 8
- Please inform me the best way to have this. 9
- Please give me a whiskey (cocktail). 10
- What about a bottle of beer and two cups? 11
- More coffee. 12
- What's for dessert? 13
- Sorry. I want to reorder my dish. 14
- This is not what we ordered. 15
- We ordered black tea, not coffee. 16
- Can I have a cup of water (some salt/pepper powder/soy sauce)? 17
- Please give me some chopsticks (a fork and knife). 18
- My salad hasn't come yet. 19
- Will my dish take much longer? 20

Paying Bills

- Let me see my bill please. **1**
- Do I pay here or at the counter? **2**
- How much is it all together? **3**
- Will a traveler's check do, too? **4**
- Can I use a credit card? **5**
- Do you charge service fees here? **6**
- Isn't there a mistake here? **7**
- Please give me an account of the items on the bill. **8**
- We'll go Dutch. **9**
- I want a formal invoice, not just a receipt. **10**

Looking for Stores

- Is there a department store nearby? **1**
- Where is the commercial area? **2**
- Are there 24-hour shops round this neighborhood? **3**
- Please tell me where I can find an art store in this city. **4**
- Are there any local product stores? **5**
- Are there any bargain shops nearby? **6**
- Are there any shops that sell cameras at affordable prices in this area? **7**
- Is there a wristwatch shop close by? **8**
- Are there any discount stores near here? **9**
- Pardon me. Could you draw a map here? **10**

Looking for Shopping Stands

- Does this shop sell handmade arts and crafts? **1**
- Where are the electronic products? **2**
- Which floor is the toyshop on? **3**
- Where are handmade arts and crafts on display? **4**
- Welcome! What would you like? **5**
- I would like to take a look at the rings. **6**
- Do you have a catalogue of products on discount? **7**
- Where is the escalator? **8**
- Where is the elevator? **9**
- Which floor are clothes for ladies on? **10**

Shopping

- I am only taking a look. **1**
- I am looking for a CD. **2**
- Do you have any recorders? **3**
- Please show me this (that). **4**
- Can I touch it? **5**
- Are these all the rings you have? **6**
- Do you have them in other styles? **7**
- Please show me your more (less) expensive ones. **8**
- Is this pure gold or plated? **9**
- Is this real? **10**

- What country of origin (brand) is this? **11**
- Is after-sales service available in France, too? **12**
- Can you take my measurement? **13**
- Can I try it on? **14**
- This material is too flowery (not flowery enough). **15**
- Do you have anything more (less) flowery? **16**
- Do you have a larger (smaller) size? **17**
- It's too big (small). It's too long (short). **18**
- It is too tight (loose). It fits me well. **19**
- Can you lower the price a little? **20**

Purchasing and Paying Bills

- It doesn't appeal to me at all. **1**
- Excuse me. I want to think it over again. **2**
- Please give me this (that) then. How much? **3**
- Please pack them separately. **4**
- Please put it in a (big) shopping bag. **5**
- Please take this credit card. **6**
- Can you send it to the US? **7**
- I haven't got my change yet. **8**
- Isn't there a mistake in your account? **9**
- There is not enough change. **10**

Looking for Tour Buses

- Where is the travel agency? **1**
- Please give me a travel service manual. **2**
- How many types of tour guides do you offer? **3**
- Do you have any city tour guides? **4**
- Are there any English (French) speaking tour guides? **5**
- When and where do we depart? **6**
- When will we get back? **7**
- What's the total cost for this (that) travel line? **8**
- Can we make reservations here? **9**
- What additional costs are there? **10**

Visiting Art Galleries and Museums

- Is it open now? **1**
- When will it be open for visitors? **2**
- When do you close? **3**
- Are there any English (French) introduction leaflets? **4**
- How much is a (child) ticket? **5**
- What is this? **6**
- Marvelous! **7**
- When was this work produced? **8**
- Who is this artist? **9**
- Is photography forbidden here? **10**

Sightseeing

- Please introduce to us some local sightseeing spots. **1**
- Let's meet here two hours from now. **2**
- When was this building built? **3**
- What's this (that)? **4**
- One moment please. I need to use the toilet. **5**
- Where can we take a sightseeing boat (funicular railway)? **6**
- Is there a coffee shop (restaurant) nearby? **7**
- Where is there a local crafts shop? **8**
- When will the bus arrive? **9**
- What time do we meet? **10**

Taking Photos

- Can I take a picture here? **1**
- Can I use the flashlight? **2**
- Is photography forbidden here (in the museum)? **3**
- Please just press here. Thank you. **4**
- Excuse us. Please take another one for us. **5**
- Do you mind taking a picture with me? **6**
- Can I take a picture of you? **7**
- I would like to send this picture to you. Could you write down your name and address here? **8**
- Please give me a 24-piece color film. **9**
- I would like B/W film. **10**

Watching Operas, Movies and Shows

- I fancy traditional art (Chinese film). 1
- Is there a service desk? 2
- Can reservations be made here? 3
- Where can I get a ticket? 4
- Where will it be performed? 5
- What performance is being put on ? 6
- When does it begin? 7
- When does it end? 8
- What hour will the next performance be performed? 9
- Where is this seat? 10

Going to Bars and Discos

- What's the most well-known dancing hall in Beijing? 1
- How much is the cover charge? 2
- Are drinks (meals) not included? 3
- Do you mind dancing with me? 4
- Is there a nightclub (bar) in this hotel? 5
- Please show me your price list. 6
- Do you have a menu with pictures? 7
- Please bring us this, this, and this. 8
- What dish is this? 9
- Please let me have two bottles of beer (zhuyeqing liquor). 10

Swimming Pool, Tennis Court, Golf Course

- Is there a swimming pool in this hotel? 1
- Are there charges for using the swimming pool? 2
- What are the costs for using your fitness club? 3
- Do you rent tennis racket? 4
- Is there a golf course nearby? 5
- Can reservations be made here? 6
- Is it far from here? 7
- How do I get there from here? 8
- Besides this, what other sports equipment is there? 9
- Are they open for use 24 hours a day? 10

Visiting a Chinese Family

- Thank you for your invitation. 1
- It is an insignificant gift. Please accept it. 2
- The house (decoration) looks very pretty. 3
- What dish is this? It's very delicious. 4
- Very good tea. 5
- I've had a pleasant day. 6
- Please visit us at our home when you come to the US. 7
- I' ve determined to study Chinese hard after I get back home. 8
- I' ll write to you immediately after I get back to the US. 9
- We'll leave now. Please don't bother to see us off. 10

Making Domestic Phone Calls

- Hi. This is Martin. Is Mr. Wang in? 1
- Who is speaking please? 2
- One moment please. 3
- Mr. Wang is not in. 4
- What time will he be back? 5
- Please ask him to call me back after he returns. 6
- My number is 61234567. 7
- I 'm in Room 108 of the Beijing Hotel. 8
- Sorry. I dialed the wrong number. 9
- Where is there a public phone? 10

Making International Phone Calls

- I want to place an international call to London, England. 1
- Please tell me your name and room number. 2
- I'm Smith and my room number is 231. 3
- What's the number you are calling? 4
- It's 0044-2078123456 in London. 5
- Mr. Wang please. 6
- Your line is through. Please speak. 7
- The line is busy. /Nobody is answering the phone. 8
- Can I call international long distance with this public phone? 9
- Please speak slowly. 10

At the Post Office

- Where is the post office? **1**
- Is there a mailbox nearby? **2**
- I want to send this letter (parcel) to France. **3**
- Please post it by air (sea). **4**
- Please send it express mail (registered). **5**
- How much is it by air (sea/express mail/registered)? **6**
- Where are stamps sold? **7**
- Please let me have a three-yuan stamp. **8**
- Where is the EMS window? **9**
- Please give me five postcards. **10**

At the Bank

- Is there a bank close by? **1**
- Please cash this traveler's check. **2**
- I want five one-hundred and five fifty notes. **3**
- Here is 2000 yuan, would you please change it into smaller bills? **4**
- Where is the foreign currency bank of the Beijing branch? **5**
- May I please ask how to go to the foreign exchange bank? **6**
- I want to change some money into RMB. Which window is it? **7**
- I want to convert all these to RMB. **8**
- How much is the exchange rate for RMB today? **9**
- Do you convert from currencies other than US dollars? **10**

Getting Lost

- Could you tell me if there is a station house nearby? **1**
- I've lost my way. Where is the Beijing Hotel? **2**
- I am a tourist from Canada. **3**
- May I bother you to write in English on my map? **4**
- Excuse me. Could you take me there? **5**
- Pardon me. Is this the way to the Beijing Railway Station? **6**
- Will this take me to the Beijing Railway Station? **7**
- Thank you for helping me . **8**
- Which is the right way? **9**
- Is it a long way on foot? **10**

Losing Things

- I lost my passport (traveler's check). **1**
- I don't know where I lost it. **2**
- I left it on the taxi. **3**
- I think someone stole it from me. **4**
- Here is the number of my traveler's check (passport). **5**
- I want to report the loss in a proper form. **6**
- I want to fill in a disembarkation confirmation form. **7**
- Where is the British embassy (consulate)? **8**
- Please contact this addresses if it is found. **9**
- Please help me find what I've lost. **10**

Theft and Fire

- Help please! **1**
- Fire!/Stop thief! **2**
- Pickpocket! **3**
- Hello! Is that the service desk? Please ask for the police. **4**
- Where is the fire extinguisher (emergency exit)? **5**
- Please take me to the nearest police station. **6**
- My purse has been stolen. **7**
- My handbag was snatched. **8**
- Please contact the embassy. **9**
- I want to talk to someone who speaks English. **10**

Traffic Accident

- One of the car's tires is flat. **1**
- There is a problem with the car. It won't move. **2**
- There has been a car accident . **3**
- Please call an ambulance quickly. **4**
- I don't speak Chinese. Please call a policeman. **5**
- Please ask for an English interpreter. **6**
- Please contact the embassy (consulate). **7**
- Will you please contact this place (person)? **8**
- I'm not responsible for this. **9**
- It's not my fault. **10**

At an Emergency

- Hello? Is that the service desk? Can someone please hurry here? **1**
- I have a horrible pain and can hardly move. **2**
- Please help me. **3**
- Please call the ambulance. **4**
- Please send for a doctor quickly. **5**
- I have a terrible stomach (tooth) ache. **6**
- Something wrong happened to me suddenly. **7**
- It's almost killing me. **8**
- Will you please contact my doctor? **9**
- Please escort me to the hospital. **10**

Seeing the Doctor

- I want to register. **1**
- I am a tourist from the US and this is my first visit to the country. **2**
- I have no reservations. I am an emergency patient. **3**
- I want to have an emergency treatment. **4**
- I want to see a doctor who speaks French (English). **5**
- I am hurt. **6**
- I broke my leg (shoulder). **7**
- I am in a very awful state. **8**
- I was in a traffic accident. **9**
- A thug suddenly attacked me. **10**

Diagnosis

· I drank a little bit too much yesterday. 1

· It feels like food poisoning. 2

· I caught a cold. 3

· My limbs feel weak and aching. 4

· I have a fever. 5

· I have a headache, a terrible headache. 6

· Loose bowels. 7

· Very nauseous. 8

· I have no appetite. 9

· I have a sore throat. 10

· I have a stopped-up nose. 11

· I cannot breathe properly. 12

· The blood type is A (AB, O). 13

· It's allergy. 14

· I have rather high (low) blood pressures. 15

· There are symptoms of diabetes. 16

· Is it serious? 17

· Can I continue to tour around? 18

· How long roughly will I be hospitalized? 19

· Please give me my diagnosis record. 20

At the Drugstores

- Have you got any medicine for colds? **1**
- I am allergic to penicillin. **2**
- Please give me some medicine for my toothache. **3**
- Do you have anything good for eye diseases? **4**
- Please give me some vitamins. **5**
- Please give me some health drinks. **6**
- Please give me some medicine for my headache (cold/diarrhea). **7**
- Please let me have some medicine for external use. **8**
- Please give me some medicine for wounds due to falls or strains. **9**
- How much are these all together? **10**

Reservation/Reconfirming Flight

- Hello. I would like to book an air ticket. **1**
- Are there vacancies on the flight from Beijing to New York in the morning of May 10th? **2**
- I want to reserve my seat on the flight from Beijing to New York. **3**
- Please reserve a seat for me on the flight in the morning of May 10th. **4**
- Please add my name to the list of passengers for seat reservation. **5**
- My name is Mike Smith. **6**
- What's the reservation number? **7**
- What is flight number, and when does it take off? **8**
- When does it arrive in New York? **9**
- I would like to reconfirm my reservation for flight 702 on US Northwest on May 10th. **10**

Changing/Canceling Flight Reservations

- I want to change my ticket scheduled for flight 702 on August 8th. **1**
- Can I change it for a flight on August 7th? **2**
- Can I change it for a morning (afternoon) flight? **3**
- I want to switch my morning flight for an afternoon one. **4**
- I want to switch my New York flight to Los Angeles. **5**
- I want to change my departure site from Beijing to Tianjin. **6**
- I want to change it for the same day. **7**
- A flight on a different airline will also do. **8**
- I want to cancel my reservation for flight 702 on August 8th. **9**
- My reservation number is 1234. **10**

Departure from China

- Where is the US Northwest airline counter? **1**
- The luggage shall be consigned by air. **2**
- Please paste a "handle with care" label on it. **3**
- Could you please give me a seat by the gate? **4**
- Please help me find my luggage quickly. **5**
- Has Northwest Airline flight 702 taken off? **6**
- Roughly what time will it arrive? **7**
- What time shall boarding begin? **8**
- Where are procedures for going abroad handled? **9**
- Could you tell me where the tax-free shop is? **10**

第1章

Basic Dialogues

Greetings

Hello!

你 好

nǐ hǎo

New Words

- greetings 问候 wèn hòu
- morning 早上 zǎo shang
- daytime 白天 bái tiān
- evening 晚上 wǎn shang
- today 今天 jīn tiān
- tomorrow 明天 míng tiān
- the day after tomorrow 后天 hòu tiān
- yesterday 昨天 zuó tiān
- the day before yesterday 前天 qián tiān

Tips

In China, people usually greet each other by saying "ní hǎo" (how do you do) or "hello", or "zǎoshàng hǎo" (good morning), "xiàwǔ hǎo" (good afternoon), "wǎnshàng hǎo" (good evening), and "wǎn ān" (good night); they say "bye-bye" just as in English. Traditional ways of greeting, such as saying "chīle ma" (have meal yet) are rarely used nowadays.

Key Sentences

1. Long time no see.

2. How is your health?

3. Very good.

4. Goodbye.

5. See you tomorrow then.

6. I have to go now.

7. No hurry.

8. You're very welcome.

9. It has been very tiring.

10. May I please ask?

应用会话 yīng yòng huì huà

1. 好久不见了。
Hǎo jiǔ bú jiàn le.

2. 你身体好吗？
Nǐ shēn tǐ hǎo ma?

3. 我很好。
Wǒ hěn hǎo.

4. 再见。
Zài jiàn.

5. 那明天见。
Nà míng tiān jiàn.

6. 那我先告辞了。
Nà wǒ xiān gào cí le.

7. 请慢走。
Qǐng màn zǒu.

8. 欢迎欢迎。
Huān yíng huān yíng.

9. 辛苦了。
Xīn kǔ le.

10. 请问。
Qǐng wèn.

Self-introduction

Nice to meet you. My name is Martin.
初次见面，我叫马丁
chū cì jiàn miàn, wǒ jiào Mǎ dīng

New Words

· self-introduction	自 我 介 绍 zì wǒ jiè shào	· civil servant	公 务 员 gōng wù yuán
· USA	美 国 Měi guó	· occupation	职 业 zhí yì
· I	我 wǒ	· name	名 字 míng zi
· tourist	游 客 yóu kè	· company	公 司 gōng sī
· college student	大 学 生 dà xué shēng	· shop	商 店 shāng diàn
· teacher	老 师 lǎo shī	· name card	名 片 míng piàn

1. Meeting in person or on the phone for the first time, you should choose the most common greeting and say "nǐ hǎo" (how do you do).
2. For a more complete self-introduction and a more pleasant trip, it is necessary to learn the sentence structures below:
   - Wǒ shì … rén (I come from...) or Wǒ jiào …(My name is...)
   - Nín shì … ma (Are you...?)
   - Wǒ yě shì … (I am..., too.)
   - Zhè shì wǒ de … (This is my...)
   - Nà shì wǒ de … (That is my...)
   - Nǐ huì shuō Yīngyǔ ma? (Do you speak English?)

Key Sentences

1. Nice to meet you.

2. My name is Martin.

3. Pleased to meet you.

4. I'll appreciate your kind consideration.

5. Here is my name card.

6. I am a tourist from the USA.

7. I am a college student (civil servant/teacher).

8. I am employed in a firm.

9. May I ask your family name?

10. May I ask what you do?

应用会话 yīng yòng huì huà

1. 初次见面。
Chū cì jiàn miàn.

2. 我叫马丁。
Wǒ jiào Mǎ dīng.

3. 见到您很高兴！
Jiàn dào nín hěn gāo xìng!

4. 请你多多关照。
Qǐng nǐ duō duō guān zhào.

5. 这是我的名片。
Zhè shì wǒ de míng piàn.

6. 我是从美国来的游客。
Wǒ shì cóng Měi guó lái de yóu kè.

7. 我是大学生（公务员、老师）。
Wǒ shì dà xué shēng (gōng wù yuán, lǎo shī).

8. 我在公司工作。
Wǒ zài gōng sī gōng zuò.

9. 请问，您贵姓？
Qǐng wèn, nín guì xìng?

10. 请问，您有什么工作？
Qǐng wèn, nín yǒu shéng me gōng zuò?

Thanks and Apologies

Thanks a lot.

非常感谢

fēi cháng gǎn xiè

New Words

· thanks	感 谢 gǎn xiè	· sincere	真 zhēn
· apologize	道 歉 dào qiàn	· trouble	麻 烦 má fan
· genial	亲 切 qīn qiè	· happy	高 兴 gāo xìng
· thank you	谢 谢 xiè xie	· It's all right.	没 关 系 méi guān xi

Tips

1. It is necessary to give presents when meeting Chinese people. The presents need not be very expensive—it is just to convey friendship and kindness; this is frequently done even between the Chinese themselves.
2. According to different situations, "xiè xie"(Thank you), or "bú kè qi" (Don't mention it)(in Chinese, this idiom is used in many cases). In response to"xiè xie"(Thank you), the phrase most frequently used by the Chinese people is "bú kè qi"(Don't mention it).
3. Duì bu qǐ (Sorry). Besides this,"láo jià"(Excuse me), and"dǎ rǎo yí xià"(Pardon) are also widely used.

Key Sentences

1. Thanks a lot.

2. My sincere thanks.

3. Thank you.

4. Thank you for all your help.

5. Don't mention it.

6. It's my pleasure.

7. I apologize.

8. I'm very sorry.

9. I've been a lot of trouble to you.

10. It's all right /no big deal.

应用会话 yīng yòng huì huà

1. 非 常 感 谢 ！
   Fēi cháng gǎn xiè!

2. 真 感 谢 你 。
   Zhēn gǎn xiè nǐ.

3. 谢 谢 。
   Xiè xie.

4. 谢 谢 您 的 关 照 。
   Xiè xie nín de guān zhào.

5. 不 要 客 气 。
   Bú yào kè qi.

6. 我 很 高 兴 帮 你 的 忙 。
   Wǒ hěn gāo xìng bāng nǐ de máng.

7. 很 抱 歉 。
   Hěn bào qiàn.

8. 对 不 起 。
   Duì bu qǐ.

9. 麻 烦 你 了 。
   Má fan nǐ le.

10. 没 关 系 。（ 没 事 儿 。）
    Méi guān xi. Méi shìr.

Uncertainty

Please say it slowly.
请您慢一点说
qǐng nín màn yì diǎn shuō

New Words

- French 法语 Fǎ yǔ
- Chinese 汉语 Hàn yǔ
- English 英语 Yīng yǔ
- Chinese characters 汉字 hàn zì
- meaning 意思 yì si
- this 这个 zhè gè
- that 那个 nà gè
- which 哪个 nǎ gè
- what time 什么时候 shénme shíhou
- she 她 tā
- he 他 tā

Tips

1. This book is compiled for tourists in China who speak little Chinese and want to express themselves and also those who don't understand Chinese at all. Each sentence is accompanied by Chinese phonetic symbols and proper intonation to help tourists speak as accurately as possible.
2. In China, a "policeman" is called "jǐngchá" or "jǐngguān". Their uniforms are dark blue and can be easily recognized anywhere.

? Key Sentences

1. Sorry. Would you please say that again?

2. Sorry. I don't understand.

3. I only speak a little Chinese.

4. Does anyone here speak English (French)?

5. How do you say this in English?

6. What's this?

7. Who is he (she)?

8. Where is it?

9. Which one is it?

10. What time?

? 应用会话 yīng yòng huì huà

1. 对不起，请您再说一遍。
   Duì bu qǐ, qǐng nín zài shuō yí biàn.

2. 对不起，我不太明白。
   Duì bu qǐ, wǒ bú tài míng bai.

3. 我会说一点儿汉语。
   Wǒ huì shuō yì diǎnr Hàn yǔ.

4. 有没有懂英语（法语）的人？
   Yǒu méi yǒu dǒng Yīng yǔ (Fǎ yǔ) de rén?

5. 这用英语怎么说？
   Zhè yòng Yīng yǔ zěn me shuō?

6. 这是什么？
   Zhè shì shén me?

7. 他（她）是谁？
   Tā (tā) shì shuí?

8. 在哪儿？
   Zài nǎr?

9. 是哪个。
   Shì nǎ gè.

10. 几点（什么时候）？
    Jǐ diǎn (shén me shí hòu)?

Affirmative/Negative Expressions

It's all right now.
好了
hǎo le

New Words

- yes 是 shì
- no 不是 bú shì
- know 知道 zhī dào
- don't know 不知道 bù zhī dào
- necessary 必要 bì yào
- good 好 hǎo
- It's all right. 没关系 méi guān xi

Tips

1. "Hǎo de,hǎo de" (OK,OK) and "méi wèntí" (no problem)are affirmative idioms frequently used in China.
2. Remember, "hǎo de, hǎo de"(OK, OK) does not always mean all is settled, there may still be "problems". Common negative expressions are:"bú shì", "méi yǒu"(no), etc.

Key Sentences

1. Yes.

2. No.

3. Fine.

4. It's all right.

5. Got it.

6. I see.

7. OK. It is settled.

8. Not necessary now.

9. I am sorry. I cannot be of help to you.

10. Is it OK?

应用会话 yīng yòng huì huà

1. 是的。
   Shì de.

2. 不是。
   Bú shì.

3. 好了。
   Hǎo le.

4. 没关系。
   Méi guān xi.

5. 知道了。
   Zhī dào le.

6. 明白了。
   Míng bai le.

7. 好，那就这样吧。
   Hǎo, nà jiù zhè yàng ba.

8. 现在不必要。
   Xiàn zài bú bì yào.

9. 对不起，我不能帮你的忙。
   Duì bu qǐ, wǒ bù néng bāng nǐ de máng.

10. 好吗？
    Hǎo ma?

Numbers and Expressions(I)

1, 2, 3, 4, 5, and 6
一 二 三 四 五 六
yī èr sān sì wǔ liù

New Words

· one	一 yī	· two	二 èr
· three	三 sān	· four	四 sì
· five	五 wǔ	· six	六 liù
· seven	七 qī	· eight	八 bā
· nine	九 jiǔ	· ten	十 shí

Tips

When an exact number is not required in speaking Chinese, the following can be used to indicate general figures: "duō", "lái", "shàngxià", or "zuǒyòu" (about), e.g. "èrshí duō" (about 20), "shí lái rén" (about 10 people), "bā gè zuǒyòu"(around 8).

Key Sentences

1. Eleven, twelve, thirteen

2. Fourteen, fifteen, sixteen

3. Seventeen, eighteen, nineteen

4. Twenty, thirty, forty

5. Fifty, sixty, seventy

6. Eighty, ninety, one hundred

7. One thousand, ten thousand, one hundred thousand

8. One million, ten million, one hundred million

9. Six thousand three hundred and forty, six thousand eight hundred and ninety

10. Three thousand six hundred and seventy-two, sixteen thousand three hundred and forty-three

应用会话 yīng yòng huì huà

1. 十一 shí yī　十二 shí èr　十三 shí sān

2. 十四 shí sì　十五 shí wǔ　十六 shí liù

3. 十七 shí qī　十八 shí bā　十九 shí jiǔ

4. 二十 èr shí　三十 sān shí　四十 sì shí

5. 五十 wǔ shí　六十 liù shí　七十 qī shí

6. 八十 bā shí　九十 jiǔ shí　一百 yì bǎi

7. 一千 yì qiān　一万 yí wàn　十万 shí wàn

8. 一百万 yì bǎi wàn　一千万 yì qiān wàn　一亿 yí yì

9. 六千三百四十 liù qiān sān bǎi sì shí　六千八百九十 liù qiān bā bǎi jiǔ shí

10. 三千六百七十二 sān qiān liù bǎi qī shí èr　一万六千三百四十三 yí wàn liù qiān sān bǎi sì shí sān

Numbers and Expressions(II)

One night, two nights, three nights, four nights, and five nights

一夜、两夜、三夜、四夜、五夜

yí yè,liǎng yè,sān yè,sì yè,wǔ yè

New Words

· one	一 个 yí gè	· room one	一 号 室 yī hào shì
· one set of	一 台 yì tái	· one person	一 个 人 yí gè rén
· one piece of	一 张 yì zhāng	· two people	两 个 人 liǎng gè rén
· one layer of	一 层 yì céng	· three people	三 个 人 sān gè rén
· one bottle of	一 瓶 yì píng	· four people	四 个 人 sì gè rén
· one cup of	一 杯 yì bēi	· five people	五 个 人 wǔ gè rén

The Chinese language makes use of a type of word which English does not—the measure word, which always appears right after the numerals to define the unit used, e.g. 一个人 yí gè rén (one person), 两间房 liǎng jiān fáng (two rooms), 十张票 shí zhāng piào(10 tickets), etc.

Key Sentences

1. One person, two people, three people, a few people

2. One, two, three, a few

3. One set of, two sets of, three sets of, several sets of

4. One basket of, two baskets of, three baskets of, a few baskets of

5. One bottle of, two bottles of, three bottles of, a few bottles of

6. One cup of, two cups of, three cups of, a few cups of

7. Room one, Room two, Room three, Room XXX

8. One copy of, two copies of, three copies of, a few copies of

9. One, two, three, a few

10. One piece of, two pieces of, three pieces of, a few pieces of

应用会话 yīng yòng huì huà

1.	一个人 yí gè rén	两个人 liǎng gè rén	三个人 sān gè rén	几个人 jǐ gè rén
2.	一个 yí gè	两个 liǎng gè	三个 sān gè	几个 jǐ gè
3.	一台 yì tái	两台 liǎng tái	三台 sān tái	几台 jǐ tái
4.	一篓 yì lǒu	二篓 èr lǒu	三篓 sān lǒu	几篓 jǐ lǒu
5.	一瓶 yì píng	两瓶 liǎng píng	三瓶 sān píng	几瓶 jǐ píng
6.	一杯 yì bēi	两杯 liǎng bēi	三杯 sān bēi	几杯 jǐ bēi
7.	一号室 yī hào shì	二号室 èr hào shì	三号室 sān hào shì	几号室 jǐ hào shì
8.	一本 yì běn	两本 liǎng běn	三本 sān běn	几本 jǐ běn
9.	一只 yì zhī	两只 liǎng zhī	三只 sān zhī	几只 jǐ zhī
10.	一张 yì zhāng	两张 liǎng zhāng	三张 sān zhāng	几张 jǐ zhāng

Time and Expressions

What time is it now?
现在几点
xiàn zài jǐ diǎn

New Words

English	Chinese	Pinyin
two fifty	两 点 五十 分	liǎng diǎn wǔ shí fēn
seven twenty	七 点 二 十 分	qī diǎn èr shí fēn
four forty-five	四 点 四 十 五 分	sì diǎn sì shí wǔ fēn
July 3rd	七 月 三 号	Qī yuè sān hào
August 14th	八 月 十 四 号	Bā yuè shí sì hào
October 9th	十 月 九 号	Shí yuè jiǔ hào
in three days	三 天 内	sān tiān nèi
one week	一 星 期	yì xīng qī
Saturday	星 期 六	Xīng qī liù
Sunday	星 期 天	Xīng qī tiān

1. When telling the month, just directly add "yuè"(the month) right after the number; when a specific date is required, add "rì" or "hào" (the date) right after the number, e.g. Christmas Day in Chinese is "12 yuè 25 rì (or hào)".
2. In Chinese, week is read "Xīng qī". Monday to Saturday are read as "Xīng qī yī, èr, sān, sì, wǔ, liù", while Sunday is different. Instead of being called "Xīng qī qī", it is "Xīng qī tiān" or "Xīng qī rì".

When talking about time, it is necessary to memorize the following expressions. The "o'clock" is read as "diǎn", so two o'clock corresponds to "liǎng diǎn"; minute is read as "fēn", e.g. 8:05 reads as "bā diǎn wǔ fēn"; a quarter is read as "kè", therefore 9:15 is "jiǔ diǎn yí kè".

Key Sentences

1. What hour, two o'clock, six o'clock, 12 o'clock

2. A few minutes, five minutes, fifteen minutes, twenty-five minutes

3. Thirty minutes, forty minutes, forty-five minutes, fifty minutes

4. Which month, January, February, March

5. September, October, November, December

6. What date, the 1st, the 4th, the 10th

7. What day, Monday, Tuesday, Wednesday

8. Thursday, Friday, Saturday, Sunday

9. Two days, three days, five days, six days

10. Several weeks, one week, two weeks

应用会话 yīng yòng huì huà

1. 几点 jǐ diǎn　两 点 liǎng diǎn　六 点 liù diǎn　十 二 点 shí èr diǎn

2. 几分 jǐ fēn　五 分 wǔ fēn　十 五 分 shí wǔ fēn　二 十 五 分 èr shí wǔ fēn

3. 三 十 分 sān shí fēn　四十 分 sì shí fēn　四十 五 分 sì shí wǔ fēn　五 十 分 wǔ shí fēn

4. 几月 jǐ yuè　一月 Yī yuè　二月 Èr yuè　三 月 Sān yuè

5. 九 月 Jiǔ yuè　十 月 Shí yuè　十 一 月 Shí yī yuè　十 二 月 Shí èr yuè

6. 几号 jǐ hào　一号 yī hào　四号 sì hào　十 号 shí hào

7. 星 期 几 xīng qī jǐ　星 期 一 Xīng qī yī　星 期 二 Xīng qī èr　星 期 三 Xīng qī sān

8. 星 期 四 Xīng qī sì　星 期 五 Xīng qī wǔ　星 期 六 Xīng qī liù　星 期 天 Xīng qī tiān

9. 两 天 liǎng tiān　三 天 sān tiān　五 天 wǔ tiān　六 天 liù tiān

10. 几个星 期 jǐ gè xīng qī　一个 星 期 yí gè xīng qī　两 个 星 期 liǎng gè xīng qī

第2章

Dialogues for Touring

Looking for Seats

Where is this seat?

这个座位在哪里

zhè gè zuò wèi zài nǎ lǐ

New Words

- airhostess 航空小姐 háng kōng xiǎo jiě
- passport 护照 hù zhào
- visa 签证 qiānzhèng
- air ticket 机票 jī piào
- seat number 座位号码 zuò wèi hào mǎ
- aisle seat 靠通道的座位 kào tōngdào de zuòwèi
- a seat in the middle 中间座位 zhōng jiān zuò wèi
- emergency exit 紧急出口 jǐn jí chū kǒu
- safety belt 安全带 ān quán dài
- passenger 乘客 chéngkè
- take off 起飞 qǐ fēi
- a boarding pass 登机牌 dēng jī pái

1. Many airlines goes to Beijing, either based in your mother country, or in China. There's no need to get nervous when taking Chinese airlines, for all the airhostesses speak English.
2. Your packages can be placed on the rack marked with the same number as your seat, or simply placed under your seat.
3. If you want to purchase the merchandise displayed on the pamphlet in the plane, reservations are needed. Fill in the application form with the flight number and time of your return flight, and you will get it when you are on your return flight.

Key Sentences

1. Good afternoon!

2. Please show me your boarding pass.

3. OK. Here is my boarding pass.

4. It's 35D.

5. Where is this seat?

6. Please walk ahead to the right (left).

7. I am sorry. Please make way for me.

8. Airhostess, the lid of the luggage trunk won't shut.

9. Excuse me , I think that 35D is my seat.

10. Would it be too much trouble for you to switch seats with him (her)?

应用会话 yīng yòng huì huà

1. 午安！/中 午好！
Wǔ ān ! / Zhōng wǔ hǎo!

2. 请给我看一下您的登机牌。
Qǐng gěi wǒ kàn yí xià nín de dēng jī pái.

3. 好的，这是我的登机牌。
Hǎo de, zhè shì wǒ de dēng jī pái.

4. 是35D
Shì sān shí wǔ D.

5. 这个座位在哪里？
Zhè gè zuò wèi zài nǎ lǐ?

6. 请 从右边（左边）往里走。
Qǐng cóng yòu biān (zuǒ biān) wǎng lǐ zǒu.

7. 对不起，请 让一下。
Duì bu qǐ, qǐng ràng yí xià.

8. 航空小姐,放行李的盖子关不上。
Háng kōng xiǎo jiě, fàng xíng lǐ de gài zi guān bu shàng.

9. 不好意思，35 D 是我的座位。
Bù hǎo yì sī, sānshíwǔD shì wǒ de zuò wèi.

10. 麻烦你，可以跟他（她）换座位吗?
Má fan nǐ, kě yǐ gēn tā (tā) huàn zuò wèi ma?

Accepting Service

Please give me a disembarkation card.

请给我入境卡

qǐng gěi wǒ rù jìng kǎ

New Words

- disembarkation card 入境卡 rù jìng kǎ
- customs declaration form 海关申报单 hǎi guān shēn bào dān
- newspaper 报纸 bào zhǐ
- magazine 杂志 zá zhì
- earphone 耳机 ěr jī
- call button 呼叫钮 hū jiào niǔ
- tighten the safety belt 系安全带 jì ān quán dài
- coffee 咖啡 kā fēi
- juice 果汁 guǒ zhī
- beer 啤酒 pí jiǔ
- water 水 shuǐ
- wine 酒 jiǔ
- perfume 香水 xiāng shuǐ

Tips for Trips

1. It takes more than 10 hours to fly from New York to Beijing.
2. During the flight, services on board, such as newspaper, magazines, food, drinks, and tax-free merchandises are provided.
3. When filling out the disembarkation card, both English and Chinese can be used. Don't forget to use beautiful handwriting.

Key Sentences

1. Coffee or black tea?

2. I would like coffee (black tea).

3. What would you care to drink?

4. I would like a beer (juice).

5. One more cup of beer, please.

6. A cup of water for me, please.

7. Can I have a piece of customs declaration form?

8. Do you have French newspapers (magazines)?

9. I would like to buy some wine and perfume.

10. May I turn the air off?

应用会话 yīng yòng huì huà

1. 你要咖啡还是红茶？
   Nǐ yào kā fēi hái shì hóng chá?

2. 我要咖啡（红茶）。
   Wǒ yào kā fēi (hóng chá).

3. 你要喝什么？
   Nǐ yào hē shén me?

4. 我要啤酒（橘汁）。
   Wǒ yào pí jiǔ (jú zhī).

5. 请再给我一杯啤酒。
   Qǐng zài gěi wǒ yì bēi pí jiǔ.

6. 请你给我一杯水。
   Qǐng nǐ gěi wǒ yì bēi shuǐ.

7. 请给我海关申报单,好吗?
   Qǐng gěi wǒ hǎi guān shēn bào dān, hǎo ma?

8. 有没有法文报纸（杂志）。
   Yǒu méi yǒu Fǎ wén bào zhǐ (zá zhì).

9. 我想买酒和香水。
   Wǒ xiǎng mǎi jiǔ hé xiāng shuǐ.

10. 可以关空调吗？
    Kě yǐ guān kōng tiáo ma?

Airsickness or Related Situations

May I ask if you carry any medicine for airsickness?

请问，有没有晕机药

qǐng wèn, yǒu méi yǒu yùn jī yào

New Words

- mood 心情 xīn qíng
- physical condition 身体情况 shēn tǐ qíng kuàng
- not so good 不好 bù hǎo
- airsickness bag 呕吐袋 ǒu tù dài
- medicine for airsickness 晕机药 yùn jī yào
- medicine 药 yào
- pillow 枕头 zhěn tou
- blanket 毯子 tǎn zi
- doctor 医生 yī shēng
- toilet 洗手间 xǐ shǒu jiān
- in use 正在使用 zhèng zài shǐ yòng

1. Medicine is provided to treat headaches, fainting, wound, etc. Besides, needlework is provided, just ask if you need it.
2. On the back of the seat in front of you, an airsickness bag is ready, use it when necessary, and ask the airhostess for water and napkins.
3. When feeling faint or having breath difficulty, the airhostess will provide you with oxygen, and help you lie in a seat for relaxation.
4. If there is a serious sick passenger, the airhostess would ask for help through the broadcasting system or the passenger list.

Key Sentences

1. My stomach is upset.

2. I am going to throw up.

3. Do you have any medicine for airsickness (headaches)?

4. Please let me have a pillow and a blanket.

5. Please give me an airsickness bag.

6. Is there a doctor here?

7. Is there a hostess here who speaks French?

8. Where is the toilet?

9. What is this medicine for?

10. I feel much better, thanks.

应用会话 yīng yòng huì huà

1. 胃不太舒服。
   Wèi bú tài shū fu.

2. 我要呕吐。
   Wǒ yào ǒu tù.

3. 有没有晕机药（头疼药）？
   Yǒu méi yǒu yùn jī yào (tóu téng yào)?

4. 请给我枕头和毯子。
   Qǐng gěi wǒ zhěn tou hé tǎn zi.

5. 请给我晕机用的袋子（呕吐袋）。
   Qǐng gěi wǒ yùn jī yòng de dài zi (ǒu tù dài).

6. 医生在吗？
   Yī shēng zài ma?

7. 哪位航空小姐会说法语？
   Nǎ wèi háng kōng xiǎo jiě huì shuō Fǎ yǔ?

8. 洗手间在哪儿？
   Xǐ shǒu jiān zài nǎr?

9. 这是什么药？
   Zhè shì shén me yào?

10. 好多了，谢谢。
    Hǎo duō le, xiè xie.

Arrival

What time do we arrive in Beijing?

几 点 到 北 京

jǐ diǎn dào Běi jīng

New Words

· destination	目 的 地 mù dì dì	· weather	天 气 tiān qì
· arrive	到 达 dào dá	· on time	正 点 zhèng diǎn
· land	降 落 jiàng luò	· luggage	行 李 xíng li
· captain	机 长 jī zhǎng	· jet lag	时 差 shí chā
· altitude	高 度 gāo dù	· local time	当 地 时 间 dāng dì shí jiān

After landing, there will be a broadcast: "Ladies and gentlemen, the plane... has arrived at the Beijing Capital International Airport. Before the plane stops completely, please keep your safety belt fastened. After the plane stops, please get out in an orderly fashion, thank you."

Key Sentences

1. Where are we flying to now?

2. Will we arrive on time?

3. What time do we get to Beijing?

4. What's the weather like in Beijing?

5. Is there any delay?

6. How long will the delay be?

7. Can I go to the toilet now?

8. Can I get up from the seat now?

9. Can I take out my luggage now?

10. It has been a tiring journey.

六 应用会话 yīng yòng huì huà

1. 现 在 正 飞 在 什 么 地 方 ?
   Xiàn zài zhèng fēi zài shén me dì fang?

2. 正 点 到 达 吗?
   Zhèng diǎn dào dá ma?

3. 几 点 到 北 京 ?
   Jǐ diǎn dào Běi jīng?

4. 北 京 的 天 气 怎 么 样 ?
   Běi jīng de tiān qì zěn me yàng?

5. 要 晚 点 吗 ?
   Yào wǎn diǎn ma?

6. 晚 点 多 长 时 间?
   Wǎn diǎn duō cháng shí jiān?

7. 现 在 可 以 去 洗 手 间 吗 ?
   Xiàn zài kě yǐ qù xǐ shǒu jiān ma?

8. 现 在 能 从 座 位 上 站 起 来 吗 ?
   Xiàn zài néng cóng zuò wèi shàng zhàn qǐ lái ma?

9. 现 在 可 以 把 行 李 拿 出 来 吗 ?
   Xiàn zài kě yǐ bǎ xíng li ná chū lái ma?

10. 辛 苦 了 。
    Xīn kǔ le.

Entry Check

I'm traveling for pleasure.

我的入境目的是观光

wǒ de rù jìng mù dì shì guān guāng

New Words

- disembarkation check 入境检查 rù jìng jiǎn chá
- stay 停留 tíng liú
- passport 护照 hù zhào
- disembarkation card 入境卡 rù jìng kǎ
- purpose 目的 mù dì
- sightseeing 观光 guān guāng
- plan 打算 dǎ suàn
- two weeks 两个星期 liǎng gè xīng qī
- business 商务 shāng wù
- liaison office 联络处 lián luò chù
- hotel 饭店 fàn diàn
- air ticket 机票 jī piào

1. Checkout and Quarantine

   Disembarking passengers shall fill in the Application for Disembarkation and Quarantine, and those who come from the epidemic-stricken areas of yellow fever must show the certificate of vaccine inoculation.

2. Border Check

   While going through disembarkation, you should keep your passport and entry visa handy; when passing through the checks, hand in your applications for entry and entrance, passport, and visa.

Key Sentences

1. How long do you plan to stay in China?

2. I will stay for one week.

3. What's your purpose of travel?

4. For pleasure (to attend business meetings).

5. What's your occupation?

6. I work in a trade company.

7. I am a student (housewife).

8. Where do you plan to stay?

9. In Beijing Hotel.

10. I haven't decided yet.

应用会话 yīng yòng huì huà

1. 您打算在中国停留多久？
   Nín dǎ suàn zài Zhōng guó tíng liú duō jiǔ?

2. 我将停留一个星期。
   Wǒ jiāng tíng liú yí gè xīng qī.

3. 您的入境目的是什么？
   Nín de rù jìng mù dì shì shén me?

4. 是来旅游（谈商务）的。
   Shì lái lǚ yóu (tán shāng wù) de.

5. 您有什么工作？
   Nín yǒu shén me gōng zuò?

6. 我在贸易公司工作。
   Wǒ zài mào yì gōng sī gōng zuò.

7. 我是学生（是家庭妇女）？
   Wǒ shì xué shēng (shì jiā tíng fù nǚ)?

8. 您打算住在哪里？
   Nín dǎ suàn zhù zài nǎ lǐ?

9. 住北京饭店。
   Zhù Běi jīng fàn diàn.

10. 还没有决定。
    Hái méi yǒu jué dìng.

Luggage Retrieval

My luggage is not yet found.
没有找到我的行李
méi yǒu zhǎo dào wǒ de xíng li

New Words

- luggage office 行李处 xíng li chù
- flight 航班 háng bān
- luggage 行李 xíng li
- flight number 航班号码 háng bān hào mǎ
- document 文件 wén jiàn
- declaration form 申报单 shēn bào dān
- name 名字 míng zi
- address 地址 dì zhǐ
- custody card 保管证 bǎo guǎn zhèng
- liaison office 联络处 lián luò chù

Tips for Trips

You can check the number of the baggage carousel that your flight is using, thus get your luggage there; if for any reason your luggage is not available; contact the airport workers and try to get information from the luggage information desk.

Key Sentences

1. Where do I get my luggage from flight 702 on US Northwest?

2. Please help me find my luggage.

3. My luggage is not yet found.

4. How many pieces of luggage do you have?

5. Two — a leather suitcase and a handbag.

6. Here is my luggage custody card.

7. Please fill in this form.

8. I've filled it in.

9. Once we find your luggage, where should we send it?

10. Please contact me at this place/number.

应用会话 yīng yòng huì huà

1. 美 西 北 702 次 航 班 在 哪 儿 取 行 李 ？
   Měi xī běi qīlíngèr cì háng bān zài nǎr qǔ xíng li?

2. 请 帮 我 找 一 找 我 的 行 李 。
   Qǐng bāng wǒ zhǎo yī zhǎo wǒ de xíng li.

3. 我 的 行 李 还 没 到 ？
   Wǒ de xíng li hái méi dào?

4. 您 有 几 件 行 李 。
   Nín yǒu jǐ jiàn xíng li?

5. 共 两 件 ，一 个 皮 箱 和 一 个 手 提 包 。
   Gòng liǎng jiàn, yí gè pí xiāng hé yí gè shǒu tí bāo.

6. 这 是 行 李 保 管 证 。
   Zhè shì xíng li bǎo guǎn zhèng.

7. 请 在 这 张 表 写 一 下 。
   Qǐng zài zhè zhāng biǎo xiě yí xià.

8. 写 好 了 。
   Xiě hǎo le.

9. 找 到 行 李 后 ，送 到 什 么 地 方 ？
   Zhǎo dào xíng li hòu, sòng dào shén me dì fang?

10. 请 联 系 这 儿 。
    Qǐng lián xì zhèr.

Customs Inspections

This is a gift for a friend.

这是送给朋友的礼物

zhè shì sòng gěi péng you de lǐ wù

New Words

- customs 海 关 hǎi guān
- check 检 查 jiǎn chá
- declare 申 报 shēn bào
- cigarette 烟 yān
- whiskey 威 士 忌 wēi shì jì
- perfume 香 水 xiāng shuǐ
- two packs 两 条 liǎng tiáo
- three bottles 三 瓶 sān píng
- handbag 手 提 包 shǒu tí bāo
- leather case 皮 箱 pí xiāng
- gift 礼 物 lǐ wù
- watch 表 biǎo
- diamond 宝 石 bǎo shí

Tips for Trips

If you aren't carrying the following items, there is no need to fill in the form, so you may go through the "Express Channel". If you are carrying these items, then you should fill out the forms and go through the "Application Channel", and put your items through the legal procedure for entry.

- ¥6,000 or above in cash, or 50g or above of gold or silver or products of these material
- Foreign currency worth $ 5,000 or above
- Plants or animals that are restricted by Chinese quarantine laws and regulations, or other items that are required for checking procedures
- Passengers unsure of the current laws and regulations should go through the "Application Channel".

Key Sentences

1. Do you have anything to declare?

2. I don't have anything to declare.

3. There is a pack of cigarettes and two bottles of wine.

4. What's in this bag?

5. Some gifts and articles of daily use.

6. Please open the leather case.

7. What's this?

8. It is a gift for a friend, a pen.

9. This watch and diamond are for my own use.

10. I bought them a year (two years/three years) ago.

应用会话 yīng yòng huì huà

1. 您有什么东西要申报吗？
   Nín yǒu shén me dōng xi yào shēn bào ma?

2. 我没有什么要申报的。
   Wǒ méi yǒu shén me yào shēn bào de.

3. 有一条烟和两瓶酒。
   Yǒu yì tiáo yān hé liǎng píng jiǔ.

4. 这个包里有什么东西?
   Zhè gè bāo lǐ yǒu shén me dōng xi?

5. 有日常用品和礼物。
   Yǒu rì cháng yòng pǐn hé lǐ wù.

6. 请打开皮箱。
   Qǐng dǎ kāi pí xiāng.

7. 这是什么东西?
   Zhè shì shén me dōng xi?

8. 这是送给朋友的礼物，是钢笔。
   Zhè shì sòng gěi péng you de lǐ wù, shì gāng bǐ.

9. 这个手表和宝石都是我自用的。
   Zhè gè shǒu biǎo hé bǎo shí dōu shì wǒ zì yòng de.

10. 都是1年（2年、3年）前买的。
    Dōu shì yì nián (liǎng nián,sān nián) qián mǎi de.

Changing Money and Taking a Bus

Which bus do I take to get to Beijing Hotel?

到北京饭店坐几路车

dào Běi jīng Fàn diàn zuò jǐ lù chē

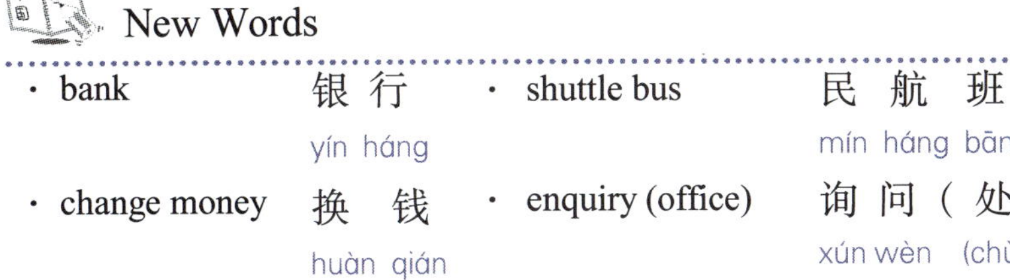

New Words

· bank	银行 yín háng	· shuttle bus	民航班车 mín háng bān chē
· change money	换钱 huàn qián	· enquiry (office)	询问（处） xún wèn (chù)
· bank note	纸币 zhǐ bì	· ticket	票 piào
· coin	硬币 yìng bì	· fly to	飞往 fēi wǎng

1. The currency in China is the RMB, one unit of which is called "yuan". Its symbol is ¥. US dollars are seldom accepted except at hotels and guesthouses.
2. It does not matter if you haven't prepared RMB before entry, for in most Chinese banks, you can change your currency directly to RMB at the counters. Some hotels and even large department stores offer this service as well. On the whole, it will not cause inconvenience.

Key Sentences

1. Where is the bank?

2. I want to change money.

3. I would like to cash my traveler's check for RMB.

4. Please give me 10 100-yuan RMB notes.

5. Please change these two hundred RMB notes to coins.

6. Where do I catch the shuttle bus?

7. Could I trouble you to go with me?

8. I'd like to buy a ticket to Qianmen (Xidan).

9. May I ask how much the fare is to Dongdan?

10. How much is a ticket to Zhongguancun?

应用会话 yīng yòng huì huà

1. 银 行 在 哪 里？
   Yín háng zài nǎ lǐ?

2. 我 要 换 钱 。
   Wǒ yào huàn qián.

3. 请 把 旅 行 支 票 换 成 人 民 币 。
   Qǐng bǎ lǚ xíng zhī piào huàn chéng rén mín bì.

4. 请 给 我 换 十 张 一 百 元 的 人 民 币 。
   Qǐng gěi wǒ huàn shí zhāng yì bǎi yuán de rén mín bì.

5. 请 把 两 百 元 人 民 币 换 成 零 钱 。
   Qǐng bǎ liǎng bǎi yuán rén mín bì huàn chéng líng qián.

6. 民 航 班 车 在 哪 儿 上？
   Mín háng bān chē zài nǎr shàng?

7. 麻 烦 你，可 以 陪 我 去 吗？
   Má fan nǐ, kě yǐ péi wǒ qù ma?

8. 请 给 我 一 张 到 前 门（西 单）的 票 。
   Qǐng gěi wǒ yì zhāng dào Qián mén (Xī dān) de piào.

9. 请 问，到 东 单 的 票 多 少 钱？
   Qǐng wèn, dào Dōng dān de piào duō shǎo qián?

10. 请 问，到 中 关 村 的 票 怎 么 买？
    Qǐng wèn, dào Zhōng guān cūn de piào zěn me mǎi?

Taking a Taxi

How much is it roughly to Xidan?

到西单大概多少钱

dào Xī dān dà gài duō shǎo qián

New Words

· taxi	出 租 车 chū zū chē	· right	右 边 yòu bian
· station	车 站 chē zhàn	· left	左 边 zuǒ bian
· fare	车 费 chē fèi	· always	一 直 yì zhí
· late at night	深 夜 shēn yè	· here	这 儿 zhèr
· stop	站 zhàn	· there	那 儿 nàr
· address	地 址 dì zhǐ	· change	找 钱 zhǎo qián
· signal	信 号 xìn hào		

Tips for Trips

1. It is a good idea to take a taxi in most Chinese cities. In Beijing for example, the prices differ according to different types of automobile. The starting cost is ¥10, which includes the fee for three kilometers; the cheapest cost is ¥1.2 per kilometer, that is, when you get in, you pay ¥10 for the first three kilometers and ¥1.2 for each additional kilometer. There are also taxis priced at ¥1.6 and ¥2 per kilometer. In Beijing, some drivers speak English; even if they don't, most of them will deliver you to your destination if you transmit the information through nonverbal means. It is true that in large cities such as Beijing, Shanghai, and Guangzhou, many residents speak English, so there is no need to worry about the problem of communication.
2. There will be many taxis waiting outside hotels and guesthouses.

 **Key Sentences**

1. May I ask where the taxi station is?
2. Could you get a taxi for me?
3. About how much is it to the Beijing Railway Station?
4. Please take me to the Beijing Railway Station.
5. Please take me to this address.
6. Please stop at the traffic lights.
7. Stop here.
8. Excuse me. Can we make a stop here?
9. Here is a one-hundred RMB note. Do you have enough change?
10. Please wait for me a little bit here.

应用会话 yīng yòng huì huà

1. 请 问，出 租 车 站 在 哪 儿？
   Qǐng wèn, chū zū chē zhàn zài nǎr?

2. 能 给 我 叫 辆 出 租 车 吗？
   Néng gěi wǒ jiào liàng chū zū chē ma?

3. 到 北 京 站 大 概 多 少 钱？
   Dào Běi jīng zhàn dà gài duō shǎo qián?

4. 请 到 北 京 站。
   Qǐng dào Běi jīng zhàn.

5. 请 到 这 个 地 址。
   Qǐng dào zhè gè dì zhǐ.

6. 请 到 红 绿 灯 那 儿 停 一 下。
   Qǐng dào hóng lǜ dēng nàr tíng yí xià.

7. 在 这 儿 停 一 下。
   Zài zhèr tíng yí xià.

8. 对 不 起，在 这 儿 停 一 下 好 吗？
   Duì bu qǐ, zài zhèr tíng yí xià hǎo ma?

9. 给 你 一 百 元 人 民 币，你 找 得 开 吗？
   Gěi nǐ yì bǎi yuán rén mín bì, nǐ zhǎo de kāi ma?

10. 请 在 这 儿 稍 等。
    Qǐng zài zhèr shāo děng.

Taking Subways / Railways

Please tell me how I can get a ticket for Xizhimen.

请告诉我怎么买西直门的票

qǐng gào su wǒ zěn me mǎi Xī zhí mén de piào

Transportation

New Words

- subway 地铁 dì tiě
- railway 铁路 tiě lù
- ticket office 售票处 shòu piào chù
- ticket examination 检票处 jiǎn piào chù
- departure 出发 chū fā
- seats with numbers coinciding with the tickets 对号座位 duì hào zuò wèi
- seats with numbers not coinciding with the tickets 不对号座位 bú duì hào zuò wèi
- return ticket 往返票 wǎng fǎn piào
- change buses 换车 huàn chē
- one-way ticket 单程票 dān chéng piào
- express train 快车 kuài chē
- carriage No. xxx 几号车 jǐ hào chē
- sleeper carriage 卧铺车 wò pù chē
- non-smoking carriage 禁烟车 jìn yān chē
- timetable 时刻表 shí kè biǎo

Tips for Trips

1. In China, there is a subway system available in Beijing, Shanghai, Guangzhou, and Tianjin.
2. With the longest lines and widest network, the Beijing subway is the best. The total length is about 95 kilometers, therefore it is very convenient to take it to get downtown. Again don't worry about the language, for at each stop there will be English announcement; additionally, in each carriage, there is the subway map, with stops labeled both in Chinese and English.
3. Trains are the most common means of transportation in China. But it is difficult to get tickets to scenic spots on festivals and holidays such as Spring Festival, May 1st Labor Day and Oct. 1st the National Day, so reservations are necessary.

Key Sentences

1. Where is the nearest subway station?

2. Where do I get off to change to the loop line?

3. How much is it roughly to Qianmen station?

4. Where do I get off to catch a bus to Qianmen station?

5. What's the next stop?

6. Is the next stop Qianmen station?

7. How many stations do we pass before I get off?

8. Could I trouble you to tell me when we get to Qianmen station?

9. Please sell me two return tickets to Xi'an.

10. Please sell me three adult tickets and one child ticket to Xi'an.

应用会话 yīng yòng huì huà

1. 什么地铁站离这儿最近？
   Shén me dì tiě zhàn lí zhèr zuì jìn?

2. 到东西线在哪儿上车？
   Dào dōng xī xiàn zài nǎr shàng chē?

3. 到前门站大概多少钱？
   Dào Qián mén zhàn dà gài duō shǎo qián?

4. 到前门站要在哪一个车站换车？
   Dào Qián mén zhàn yào zài nǎ yí gè chē zhàn huàn chē?

5. 下站是什么站？
   Xià zhàn shì shén me zhàn?

6. 下站是前门站吗？
   Xià zhàn shì Qián mén zhàn ma?

7. 从这儿起到第几站下车好呢？
   Cóng zhèr qǐ dào dì jǐ zhàn xià chē hǎo ne?

8. 麻烦你，到前门站告我一声好吗？
   Má fan nǐ, dào Qián mén zhàn gào wǒ yì shēng hǎo ma?

9. 请给我两张西安的往返票？
   Qǐng gěi wǒ liǎng zhāng Xī' ān de wǎng fǎn piào?

10. 请给我到西安的，三张大人票，一张小孩票。
    Qǐng gěi wǒ dào Xī' ān de, sān zhāng dà rén piào, yì zhāng xiǎo hái piào.

Key Sentences

11. How much is a return ticket?

12. Is there an express train?

13. Does the express train stop at Xi'an station?

14. Which platform does the train for Shanghai depart from?

15. May I know if this seat is occupied?

16. May I smoke here?

17. I am sorry. I lost my ticket.

18. Sorry, I missed my stop.

19. Could I get this ticket returned to you?

20. Please give me a timetable.

11. 往 返 票 多 少 钱?
Wǎng fǎn piào duō shǎo qián?

12. 有 没 有 快 车?
Yǒu méi yǒu kuài chē?

13. 快 车 到 西安 站 停 吗?
Kuài chē dào Xī'ān zhàn tíng ma?

14. 去 上 海 从几号 站 台发车?
Qù Shàng hǎi cóng jǐ hào zhàn tái fā chē?

15. 请 问,这 个 座 位 有 人 吗?
Qǐng wèn,zhè gè zuò wèi yǒu rén ma?

16. 在 这 儿 可 以 吸 烟 吗 ?
Zài zhèr kě yǐ xī yān ma?

17. 对 不 起 ,我 丢 了 车 票 。
Duì bu qǐ, wǒ diū le chē piào.

18. 对 不 起 ,我 坐 过 站 了 。
Duì bu qǐ, wǒ zuò guò zhàn le.

19. 可 以 给 我 退 掉 这 张 票 吗 ?
Kě yǐ gěi wǒ tuì diào zhè zhāng piào ma?

20. 请 给 我 时 刻 表 。
Qǐng gěi wǒ shí kè biǎo.

Taking Buses

Does this bus go to Tian'anmen Square?

这个公共汽车到天安门广场吗

zhè gè gōng gòng qì chē dào Tiān'ān mén Guǎng chǎng ma

New Words

- bus 公共汽车 gōng gòng qì chē
- shuttle bus 民航班车 mín háng bān chē
- long distance bus 长途汽车 cháng tú qì chē
- bus station 汽车站 qì chē zhàn
- change 找钱 zhǎo qián
- bus station 车站 chē zhàn
- bus ticket 车票 chē piào
- change 零钱 líng qián

Tips for Trips

1. In China, transliteration is almost always used with imported items, e.g. Coca-Cola reads "kě-kǒu-kě-lè".
2. Bus costs differ in various Chinese cities, but on the whole, they are the cheapest choice. In Beijing, most urban buses cost one yuan without air conditioning, and those with air conditioning cost two yuan. Ticket prices increase with the distance traveled, but all buses within the Fourth Ring Road will never cost more than five yuan.
3. There is some inconvenience in taking buses, that is, Chinese is required to some extent. What's more, they are usually so crowded that you are likely to get off at the wrong stop.

Key Sentences

1. Is there a bus to Xidan nearby?

2. Where do I get on a bus to Xidan?

3. Which bus do I take to the Beijing Railway Station?

4. Which bus will take me to the Beijing Railway Station area?

5. Does this bus go to the Beijing Railway Station?

6. How long will I have to wait for the next bus?

7. About how long does it take to get to the Beijing Station?

8. How many stations are there from here to the Beijing Railway Station?

9. May I trouble you to tell me when we get to the Beijing Railway Station?

10. Sorry, I have no change.

应用会话 yīng yòng huì huà

1. 附近有没有到西单的公共汽车？
Fù jìn yǒu méi yǒu dào Xī dān de gōng gòng qì chē?

2. 在哪儿坐到西单的公共汽车。
Zài nǎr zuò dào Xī dān de gōng gòng qì chē.

3. 到北京站坐几路车?
Dào Běi jīng zhàn zuò jǐ lù chē?

4. 坐几路汽车能到北京站附近？
Zuò jǐ lù qì chē néng dào Běi jīng zhàn fù jìn?

5. 这路汽车去不去北京站？
Zhè lù qì chē qù bú qù Běi jīng zhàn?

6. 这路汽车多长时间来一趟?
Zhè lù qì chē duō cháng shí jiān lái yí tàng?

7. 去北京站大约需多长时间?
Qù Běi jīng zhàn dà yuē xū duō cháng shí jiān?

8. 从这站到北京站是第几站?
Cóng zhè zhàn dào Běi jīng zhàn shì dì jǐ zhàn?

9. 麻烦你，到了北京站请告诉我。
Má fan nǐ, dào le Běi jīng zhàn qǐng gào su wǒ.

10. 对不起，我没有零钱。
Duì bu qǐ, wǒ méi yǒu líng qián.

Renting a Car

I would like to rent a car.

我想租小汽车

wǒ xiǎng zū xiǎo qì chē

New Words

- price listings 价格表 jià gé biǎo
- catalogue 目录表 mù lù biǎo
- insurance 保险 bǎo xiǎn
- gasoline 汽油 qì yóu
- gas station 加油站 jiā yóu zhàn
- international driver's license 国际驾驶执照 guó jì jià shǐ zhí zhào
- driving map 交通地图 jiāo tōng dì tú
- rental fee 租价 zū jià
- highway 高速公路 gāo sù gōng lù
- toll roads 收费道路 shōu fèi dào lù
- fill up with gas 加满油 jiā mǎn yóu

1. Remember to ask for a receipt after taking a taxi in China, in order to avoid trouble if you lose some belongings .
2. The rents vary if you hire a taxi by the day for urban touring. In Beijing, it costs about ¥300~ 500 for a taxi priced at ¥1.2 per kilometer; while one that costs ¥1.6 per kilometer, will charge ¥500~700 for a whole day.

Key Sentences

1. I would like to rent a car.

2. Here is my international driver's license.

3. Show me your price listings.

4. Do you have a car catalogue?

5. Do you have a 2,000-ml. auto car?

6. I would like to have this one.

7. Do you want insurance?

8. Is gasoline included?

9. What's the best way to contact you in case of an accident?

10. Do you have a foreign language (French) driving map?

应用会话 yīng yòng huì huà

1. 我想租小汽车。
   Wǒ xiǎng zū xiǎo qì chē.

2. 这是我的国际驾驶执照。
   Zhè shì wǒ de guó jì jià shǐ zhí zhào.

3. 给我看一下价格表。
   Gěi wǒ kàn yí xià jià gé biǎo.

4. 有没有车的目录表?
   Yǒu méi yǒu chē de mù lù biǎo?

5. 有没有 2.0 的自动挡轿车?
   Yǒu méi yǒu èr diǎn líng de zì dòng dǎng jiào chē?

6. 我要这辆车。
   Wǒ yào zhè liàng chē.

7. 买不买保险?
   Mǎi bù mǎi bǎo xiǎn?

8. 不包括汽油费吗?
   Bù bāo kuò qì yóu fèi ma?

9. 有事故时,该怎么跟你联系?
   Yǒu shì gù shí, gāi zěn me gēn nǐ lián xì?

10. 有没有外文(法文)的交通地图?
    Yǒu méi yǒu wài wén (Fǎ wén) de jiāo tōng dì tú?

Reserving a Room

Is there a clean and inexpensive hotel?

有没有又便宜又干净的饭店

yǒu méi yǒu yòu pián yi yòu gān jìng de fàn diàn

New Words

- hotel 饭店 fàn diàn
- rest house 招待所 zhāo dài suǒ
- youth hostel 青年招待所 qīng nián zhāo dài suǒ
- book 预订 yù dìng
- travel agency 旅行社 lǚ xíng shè
- stay for one night 住一夜 zhù yí yè
- room 房间 fáng jiān
- spare room 空间 kōng jiān
- room rate 房价 fáng jià
- with a bathroom 带浴室 dài yù shì

Tips for Trips

1. Just like most other countries, hotels in China are ranked by the number of stars. The price of a hotel is reflected in the number of stars.
2. In Chinese, the word "hotel" can be expressed in many ways, such as "…fàndiàn", "…bīnguǎn", "…dàjiǔdiàn". To save money, booking rooms through travel agencies is much cheaper, generally with a discount of 30%, or even 50% in the slack season.

Key Sentences

1. Where is the travel agency?

2. Can I book a room in the Beijing Hotel here?

3. Please help me find a clean and inexpensive hotel.

4. I would like something near the Beijing Railway Station (Airport) area.

5. How many minutes does it take on foot from the Beijing Railway Station?

6. I would like a room for less than 500 RMB per day.

7. I would like to book a room in the Youth Hostel.

8. Please refer me to some other hotels.

9. Is there a more economical hotel (room)?

10. How much is it per person each day?

应用会话 yīng yòng huì huà

1. 旅 行 社 在 哪 里 ?
Lǚ xíng shè zài nǎ lǐ?

2. 在 这 里可以预 订 北 京 饭 店 吗?
Zài zhè lǐ kě yǐ yù dìng Běi jīng Fàn diàn ma?

3. 请 介 绍 一下 又 便 宜又 干 净的 饭 店。
Qǐng jiè shào yí xià yòu pián yi yòu gān jìng de fàn diàn.

4. 我觉得北京 站 (机场) 附近好。
Wǒ jué de Běi jīng zhàn (jī chǎng) fù jìn hǎo.

5. 从 火 车 站 , 走 路 要 几 分 钟 ?
Cóng huǒ chē zhàn,zǒu lù yào jǐ fēn zhōng?

6. 我 要 一 天 不 到 五 百 人 民 币 的 房 间 。
Wǒ yào yì tiān bú dào wǔ bǎi Rén mín bì de fáng jiān.

7. 我 要 预 订 青 年 招 待 所 。
Wǒ yào yù dìng qīng nián zhāo dài suǒ.

8. 请 介 绍 一 下 别 的 饭 店 。
Qǐng jiè shào yí xià bié de fàn diàn.

9. 有 没 有 更 便宜一 点儿的 饭 店(房间)?
Yǒu méi yǒu gèng pián yi yì diǎnr de fàn diàn (fáng jiān)?

10. 一 个 人 一 天 多 少 钱 ?
Yí gè rén yì tiān duō shǎo qián?

Check-in/Check-out

Yes, it has already been booked.

是的，已经预订好了

shì de, yǐ jīng yù dìng hǎo le

New Words

- room 住房 zhù fáng
- room card 住房卡 zhù fáng kǎ
- single room 单人房 dān rén fáng
- double room 双人房 shuāng rén fáng
- breakfast included 包括早餐 bāo kuò zǎo cān
- traveler's check 旅行支票 lǚ xíng zhī piào
- valuables 贵重物品 guì zhòng wù pǐn
- check-out 退房 tuì fáng
- book 预订 yù dìng
- service fee 服务费 fú wù fèi
- down payment 订金 dìng jīn
- porter 行李员 xíng lǐ yuán
- service desk 服务台 fú wù tái

Tips for Trips

1. In China, a deposit is usually required on top of the room rental costs, and this will be returned to you after you check out.
2. In addition, a tip is a must in some cases. If someone declines to accept your tip, it is a good idea to leave ¥10~20 under the pillow or in another place where it will be easy to find.

Key Sentences

1. My name is Mike. My room is booked in advance in New York.

2. It was booked at the airport (travel agency).

3. I want a single (double) room.

4. Is service fee (tax) included?

5. Does the room rate include breakfast?

6. Is a reservation required for breakfast?

7. Please leave these valuables at the service desk.

8. Please take my luggage to my room.

9. I would like a very quiet room.

10. Excuse me, please let me have a room with a view.

应用会话 yīng yòng huì huà

1. 我叫迈克，在纽约已经预订好了。
   Wǒ jiào Mài kè, zài Niǔ yuē yǐ jīng yù dìng hǎo le.

2. 在机场（旅行社）预订了。
   Zài jī chǎng (lǚ xíng shè) yù dìng le.

3. 我要单人房（双人房）。
   Wǒ yào dān rén fáng (shuāng rén fáng).

4. 包括服务费（税金）吗？
   Bāo kuò fú wù fèi (shuì jīn) ma?

5. 这房费包括早餐吗?
   Zhè fáng fèi bāo kuò zǎo cān ma?

6. 吃早餐需要预订吗？
   Chī zǎo cān xū yào yù dìng ma?

7. 请把这些贵重物品存到服务台。
   Qǐng bǎ zhè xiē guì zhòng wù pǐn cún dào fú wù tái.

8. 请把我的行李送到房间去。
   Qǐng bǎ wǒ de xíng lǐ sòng dào fáng jiān qù.

9. 我要很安静的房间。
   Wǒ yào hěn ān jìng de fáng jiān.

10. 拜托，给我间风景好的房间。
    Bài tuō, gěi wǒ jiān fēng jǐng hǎo de fáng jiān.

Key Sentences

11. Can I take a look at the room?

12. I would like to check out now.

13. When is the latest check-out time?

14. I would like to stay for one more day.

15. I would like to check out one day earlier. Is that all right with you?

16. Do you take traveler's checks (credit cards)?

17. I want to leave my valuables with you.

18. Could you call the porter for me?

19. Would you get a taxi for me?

20. Where is the shuttle bus ?

11. 可 以 看 一 下 房 间 吗 ?
Kě yǐ kàn yí xià fáng jiān ma?

12. 我 想 现 在 就 退 房 。
Wǒ xiǎng xiàn zài jiù tuì fáng.

13. 可 以 到 几 点 退 房 ?
Kě yǐ dào jǐ diǎn tuì fáng?

14. 我 还 要 住 一 天 。
Wǒ hái yào zhù yì tiān.

15. 我 想 早 一 天 退 房 , 可 以 吗 ?
Wǒ xiǎng zǎo yì tiān tuì fáng, kě yǐ ma?

16. 你 们 接 受 旅 行 支 票 (信 用 卡) 吗 ?
Nǐ men jiē shòu lǚ xíng zhī piào (xìn yòng kǎ) ma?

17. 我 把 贵 重 物 品 存 到 你 们 那 儿 。
Wǒ bǎ guì zhóng wù pǐn cún dào nǐ men nàr.

18. 请 叫 行 李 员 来 好 吗 ?
Qǐng jiào xíng lǐ yuán lái hǎo ma?

19. 请 你 叫 出 租 车 好 吗 ?
Qǐng nǐ jiào chū zū chē hǎo ma?

20. 在 哪 儿 坐 民 航 班 车 ?
Zài nǎr zuò mín háng bān chē?

Complaint

What's the voltage of the electricity in this hotel?

这个饭店的电压是多少

zhè gè fàn diàn de diàn yā shì duō shǎo

New Words

- door 门 mén
- key 钥匙 yào shi
- air conditioning 空调 kōng tiáo
- heating 暖气 nuǎn qì
- hot water 热水 rè shuǐ
- towel 毛巾 máo jīn
- toothbrush 牙刷 yá shuā
- bathroom 浴室 yù shì
- lavatory 洗脸间 xǐ liǎn jiān
- TV 电视机 diàn shì jī
- reading lamp 台灯 tái dēng
- problem 故障 gù zhàng
- soap 肥皂 féi zào

Tips for Trips

1. A hair drier is available in most hotels.
2. If laundry or other services are needed, make a phone call to the information desk.
3. Try to use the following routine phrases:

·Zhè shì … fángjiān.Qǐng gěi wǒ ná shuāng tuōxié hǎo ma? (This is Room No. …, would you please bring me a pair of slippers?)

·Try replacing "tuōxié" (slippers) with ①"máojīn" (towel) ② "kāishuǐ" (boiled water) ③ "yījià" (clothes rack) for exercises.

Complaint

Key Sentences

1. Excuse me. I am not satisfied with this room. May I change to another room?

2. The room key is broken.

3. I left my key in my room.

4. Maybe the air conditioning (heat) has broken down.

5. Please adjust the air to make this room warmer.

6. There is no hot water in the bathroom.

7. There is no towel (soap).

8. The light in the room (bathroom) is broken.

9. The TV (reading lamp) won't work.

10. There is no tap water in the lavatory (The tap water in the lavatory runs nonstop).

应用会话 yīng yòng huì huà

1. 麻烦你，我不满意这间房间，可以换吗？
   Má fan nǐ, wǒ bù mǎn yì zhè jiān fáng jiān, kě yǐ huàn ma?

2. 房间的钥匙坏了。
   Fáng jiān de yào shi huài le.

3. 我把钥匙留在房间里了。
   Wǒ bǎ yào shi liú zài fáng jiān lǐ le.

4. 可能空调（暖气）坏了吧。
   Kě néng kōng tiáo (nuǎn qì) huài le ba.

5. 请把房间调暖和些吧。
   Qǐng bǎ fáng jiān tiáo nuǎn huo xiē ba.

6. 浴室里不出热水。
   Yù shì lǐ bù chū rè shuǐ.

7. 没有毛巾（肥皂）。
   Méi yǒu máo jīn (féi zào).

18. 房间（浴室）里的电灯不亮。
    Fáng jiān (yù shì) lǐ de diàn dēng bú liàng.

19. 电视机（台灯）坏了。
    Diàn shì jī (tái dēng) huài le.

20. 洗手间水流不出来（流着不停）。
    Xǐ shǒu jiān shuǐ liú bù chū lái (liú zhe bù tíng).

Asking for Services

A lot of hard work on your part.
真辛苦了
zhēn xīn kǔ le

New Words

- room service 客房服务 kè fáng fú wù
- for one person 一人份 yì rén fèn
- for two people 两人份 liǎng rén fèn
- wake-up call 叫早服务 jiào zǎo fú wù
- clean up 打扫 dǎ sǎo
- photocopy 复印 fù yìn
- facsimile 传真 chuán zhēn
- coffee shop 咖啡厅 kā fēi tīng
- lunch 午饭 wǔ fàn
- supper 晚饭 wǎn fàn
- coffee 咖啡 kā fēi
- black tea 红茶 hóng chá
- leave a message 留言 liú yán
- the barber's 理发厅 lǐ fà tīng
- dry cleaning 干洗 gān xǐ

Tips for Trips

When you need service in either a hotel or a restaurants, you can just call "fú wù yuán"(waiter) no matter whether the person is male or female.

Key Sentences

1. Please send me two sandwiches and two cups of tomato juice.

2. I'm in room 505, and I would like some ice and water.

3. I would like to have breakfast in my room.

4. When does the coffee shop open (close)?

5. Please wake me up at 6 o'clock tomorrow morning.

6. Are there any messages for me?

7. Pardon me. Please send me one more quilt (bath towel).

8. Do you provide fax services?

9. Please have this jacket dry cleaned (ironed).

10. Please clean up the room.

应用会话 yīng yòng huì huà

1. 请 给 我 送来 两 人份的 三明 治和 两 杯西红柿汁。
Qǐng gěi wǒ sòng lái liǎng rén fèn de sānmíngzhì hé liǎng bēi xīhóngshìzhī.

2. 这里是 505 号,请 给我 拿来一些 冰 块 和水。
Zhè lǐ shì wǔ líng wú hào,qǐng gěi wǒ ná lái yì xiē bīng kuài hé shuǐ.

3. 我 要在 房 间里吃 早 饭。
Wǒ yào zài fáng jiān lǐ chī zǎo fàn.

4. 咖啡厅几点 开(关)门?
Kā fēi tīng jǐ diǎn kāi(guān)mén?

5. 请 在 明 天 早 上 六 点 钟 叫 醒 我。
Qǐng zài míng tiān zǎo shang liù diǎn zhōng jiào xǐng wǒ.

6. 有 我 的 留 言 吗 ?
Yǒu wǒ de liú yán ma?

7. 拜 托 ,请 送 我 另 一 床 被(一条 浴 巾)。
Bài tuō, qǐng sòng wǒ lìng yì chuáng bèi (yì tiáo yù jīn).

8. 有 没 有 发 传 真 的服 务?
Yǒu méi yǒu fā chuán zhēn de fú wù?

9. 请 把 这 件衣服 干洗(熨)一下。
Qǐng bǎ zhè jiàn yī fu gān xǐ (yùn) yí xià.

10. 请 打 扫 房 间 。
Qǐng dǎ sǎo fáng jiān.

Looking for Restaurants

Please recommend a restaurant that offers delicious food at reasonable prices.

请介绍一下味道
又好又便宜的餐厅

qǐng jiè shào yí xià wèi dào
yòu hǎo yòu pián yi de cān tīng

New Words

- restaurant 餐厅 cān tīng
- dine 吃饭 chī fàn
- book/reserve 预订 yù dìng
- introduce 介绍 jiè shào
- Chinese cuisine 中国菜 Zhōng guó cài
- dishes with local flavors 地方风味菜 dì fāng fēng wèi cài
- Shandong cuisine 山东菜 Shān dōng cài
- Sichuan cuisine 四川菜 Sì chuān cài
- good taste 味道好 wèi dào hǎo

1. In China, restaurants in downtown area tend to have a more magnificent appearance than those in other places.
2. Many kinds of names are used according to the size of restaurants, such as "~diàn", "~cāntīng", and "~lóu".
3. In Beijing, you can try flavors of different areas. For example, Donghuamen night market, which is famous for snacks.

Key Sentences

1. Is there any place nearby where we can eat?

2. Is there a restaurant which serves Western food near here?

3. Are there any restaurants with a local flavor in this area?

4. Are there any hotels that offer reasonably priced food near here?

5. Do you know of any inexpensive eateries around here?

6. Any other restaurants?

7. I would like to book a table for 7 p.m. today (tomorrow).

8. Is a suit mandatory?

9. I would like to book a private room.

10. Please let me have a seat by the window.

应用会话 yīng yòng huì huà

1. 附近有没有吃饭的地方？
   Fù jìn yǒu méi yǒu chī fàn de dì fang?

2. 附近有没有西餐厅？
   Fù jìn yǒu méi yǒu xī cān tīng?

3. 附近有没有地方风味餐厅？
   Fù jìn yǒu méi yǒu dì fāng fēng wèi cān tīng?

4. 附近有没有不太贵的饭店？
   Fù jìn yǒu méi yǒu bú tài guì de fàn diàn?

5. 附近有没有便宜一点儿的餐厅？
   Fù jìn yǒu méi yǒu pián yi yì diǎnr de cān tīng?

6. 有没有别的餐厅？
   Yǒu méi yǒu bié de cān tīng?

7. 我要预订今天(明天) 晚上 7点的饭。
   Wǒ yào yù dìng jīn tiān(míng tiān) wǎn shang qī diǎn de fàn.

8. 不穿西服也可以吗?
   Bù chuān xī fú yě kě yǐ ma?

9. 我想预订包间。
   Wǒ xiǎng yù dìng bāo jiān.

10. 请给我靠窗的座位。
    Qǐng gěi wǒ kào chuāng de zuò wèi.

At the Gate of a Restaurant

Can I sit over there by the window?

可以坐那边靠窗户的座位吗

kě yǐ zuò nà biān kào chuāng hu de zuò wèi ma

New Words

reserve a seat	定座 dìng zuò	how many people	几位 jǐ wèi
waiter	服务员 fú wù yuán	one person	一个人 yí gè rén
waitress	女服务员 nǚ fú wù yuán	two people	两个人 liǎng gè rén
window	橱窗 chú chuāng	group	团体 tuán tǐ
seat	座位 zuò wèi	room	房间 fáng jiān

Tips for Trips

1. The waiters at the door of medium or larger restaurants will lead you to your seats.
2. After settling down, the waiters will offer you tea and menu.
3. The Chinese drink a variety of teas, mainly green tea, jasmine tea, chrysanthemum tea, and longjing tea.

Key Sentences

1. My name is Martin, and I have booked a table for 7:30.

2. Welcome. Do you have a reservation?

3. Yes.

4. No. Are there any tables available?

5. How many of you are there?

6. There are four of us.

7. Please wait a moment.

8. How long will we have to wait?

9. How do you like these seats?

10. Fine. They are OK. Thanks.

应用会话 yīng yòng huì huà

1. 我叫马丁，已经预订了七点半的饭。
   Wǒ jiào Mǎ dīng ,yǐ jīng yù dìng le qī diǎn bàn de fàn.

2. 欢迎光临，您预订了吗？
   Huān yíng guāng lín, nín yù dìng le ma?

3. 是的。
   Shì de.

4. 没有，有座位吗？
   Méi yǒu, yǒu zuò wèi ma?

5. 请问，几位？
   Qǐng wèn, jǐ wèi?

6. 四个人。
   Sì gè rén.

7. 请稍等。
   Qǐng shāo děng.

8. 等多久呢？
   Děng duō jiǔ ne?

9. 这边座位怎么样。
   Zhè biān zuò wèi zěn me yàng?

10. 好，没关系的，谢谢。
    Hǎo, méi guān xì de, xiè xie.

Ordering a Meal and Other Requests

Can you bring me a spoon?

请拿勺子来好吗

qǐng ná sháo zi lái hǎo ma

New Words

· order dishes	点 菜 diǎn cài	· roasted bread	烤 面 包 kǎo miàn bāo
· menu	菜 单 cài dān	· cheese	奶 酪 nǎi lào
· plate	盘 子 pán zi	· cake	蛋 糕 dàn gāo
· rice	饭 fàn	· fruit	水 果 shuǐ guǒ
· bread	面 包 miàn bāo	· sandwich	三 明 治 sān míng zhì
· jam	果 酱 guǒ jiàng	· fried beefsteak	炸 牛 排 zhá niú pái

Tips for Trips

1. Raise your hands and call "fú wù yuán" (waiter), "xiǎo jiě" (miss) or "xiān sheng" (mister) in need.
2. In China, the atmosphere of a meal is much more important than the dinner itself, so you don't have to hurry ; instead, eat slowly to your heart's content, as the dishes will be offered one at a time. Rushing through a meal may cause you to lose your appetite, which would be a pity.

Key Sentences

1. What would you like to order?

2. Please show me your menu.

3. What dish is this?

4. Tell us about your chef's specialties today.

5. What dish can be made the fastest?

6. What dishes are not cooked with pork (chicken/beef)?

7. I would like a vegetable (cream) soup.

8. Please grill mine rare (well-done).

9. Please inform me the best way to have this.

10. Please give me a whiskey (cocktail).

应用会话 yīng yòng huì huà

1. 您来点儿什么？
Nín lái diǎnr shén me?

2. 请把菜单给我看看。
Qǐng bǎ cài dān gěi wǒ kàn kan.

3. 这是什么菜？
Zhè shì shén me cài?

4. 介绍一下今天的拿手菜？
Jiè shào yí xià jīn tiān de ná shǒu cài?

5. 什么菜上得最快？
Shén me cài shàng de zuì kuài?

6. 没有猪（鸡、牛）肉的菜是什么菜？
Méi yǒu zhū (jī, niú) ròu de cài shì shén me cài?

7. 我要蔬菜汤（奶油汤）。
Wǒ yào shū cài tāng (nǎi yóu tāng).

8. 请烤嫩一点儿（三分熟、老一点儿）。
Qǐng kǎo nèn yì diǎnr (sān fēn shú、lǎo yì diǎnr).

9. 请告诉我怎么吃好。
Qǐng gào su wǒ zěn me chī hǎo.

10. 请给我一杯威士忌（鸡尾酒）。
Qǐng gěi wǒ yì bēi wēi shì jì (jī wěi jiǔ).

11. What about a bottle of beer and two cups?

12. More coffee.

13. What's for dessert?

14. Sorry. I want to reorder my dish.

15. This is not what we ordered.

16. We ordered black tea, not coffee.

17. Can I have a cup of water (some salt/pepper powder/ soy sauce)?

18. Please give me some chopsticks (a fork and knife).

19. My salad hasn't come yet .

20. Will my dish take much longer?

11. 来一瓶啤酒和两个杯子好吗?
Lái yì píng pí jiǔ hé liǎng gè bēi zi hǎo ma?

12. 再来杯咖啡。
Zài lái bēi kā fēi.

13. 有什么甜食?
Yǒu shén me tián shí?

14. 对不起,我要换一下我点的菜。
Duì bu qǐ, wǒ yào huàn yí xià wǒ diǎn de cài.

15. 这不是我们点的。
Zhè bú shì wǒ men diǎn de.

16. 点的不是咖啡,是红茶。
Diǎn de bú shì kā fēi, shì hóng chá.

17. 来一杯水(一些盐、胡椒粉、酱油)好吗?
Lái yì bēi shuǐ (yì xiē yán, hú jiāo fěn, jiàng yóu) hǎo ma?

18. 请拿筷子(叉子、刀子)来。
Qǐng ná kuài zi (chā zi、dāo zi) lái.

19. 沙拉还没来。
Shā lā hái méi lái.

20. 我点的菜还要等吗?
Wǒ diǎn de cài hái yào děng ma?

Paying Bills

Can I pay the bill with this credit card?

可以用这张信用卡结账吗

kě yǐ yòng zhè zhāng xìn yòng kǎ jié zhàng ma

New Words

· pay a bill	结 账 jié zhàng	· card	卡 kǎ
· counter	柜 台 guì tái	· service fee	服 务 费 fú wù fèi
· how much	多 少 duō shǎo	· go Dutch	各付各的 gè fù gè de
· cash	现 金 xiàn jīn	· a simple receipt	简 单 的 收 据 jiǎn dān de shōu jù
		· receipt	收 据 shōu jù

Tips for Trips

1. Restaurants do not accept credit cards, except for those that mainly serve foreigners.
2. You could go directly to the counter to pay with cash, or stay in your seat and call the waiters to you.

Key Sentences

1. Let me see my bill please.

2. Do I pay here or at the counter?

3. How much is it all together?

4. Will a traveler's check do, too?

5. Can I use a credit card?

6. Do you charge service fees here?

7. Isn't there a mistake here?

8. Please give me an account of the items on the bill.

9. We'll go Dutch.

10. I want a formal invoice, not just a receipt.

应用会话 yīng yòng huì huà

1. 请 拿 账 单 来 。
   Qǐng ná zhàng dān lái.

2. 在 这 儿 算 账 ， 还 是 在 柜 台 算 账 ？
   Zài zhèr suàn zhàng, hái shì zài guì tái suàn zhàng?

3. 一 共 多 少 钱 ？
   Yí gòng duō shǎo qián?

4. 旅 行 支 票 也 可 以 吗 ？
   Lǚ xíng zhī piào yě kě yǐ ma?

5. 可 以 用 信 用 卡 吗 ？
   Kě yǐ yòng xìn yòng kǎ ma?

6. 这 里 收 服 务 费 吗 ？
   Zhè lǐ shōu fú wù fèi ma?

7. 这 是 不 是 算 错 了 ？
   Zhè shì bú shì suàn cuò le?

8. 请 说 明 账 单 项 目 。
   Qǐng shuō míng zhàng dān xiàng mù.

9. 我 们 要 各 付 各 的 。
   Wǒ men yào gè fù gè de.

10. 我 不 要 简 单 的 收 据 ， 要 正 式 的 发 票 。
    Wǒ bú yào jiǎn dān de shōu jù, yào zhèng shì de fā piào.

Looking for Stores

Please tell me which shop sells cameras at affordable prices.

请告诉我哪家商店的照相机便宜

qǐng gào su wǒ nǎ jiā shāng diàn de zhào xiàng jī pián yi

New Words

- department store 百货商店 bǎi huò shāng diàn
- commercial area 商业区 shāng yè qū
- bookstore 书店 shū diàn
- stationery store 文具店 wén jù diàn
- bakery 面包店 miàn bāo diàn
- florist 花店 huā diàn
- toyshop 玩具店 wán jù diàn
- grocery 食品商店 shí pǐn shāng diàn
- cosmetics store 化妆品商店 huà zhuāng pǐn shāng diàn
- jewelry store 珠宝商店 zhū bǎo shāng diàn
- sports store 体育用品店 tǐ yù yòng pǐn diàn
- local product shop 土产商店 tǔ chǎn shāng diàn

Tips for Trips

1. If you choose not to visit the Great Wall, shopping at Xiushui Street in Beijing is a tradition for visitors to China. It is a market in the open air, filled with vendors and customers. Although the atmosphere may be somewhat more chaotic than department stores, all the tourists love to come. Almost all the vendors speak some English, so communication is not a problem. Besides, merchandise is abundant here, from the silk loved by the westerners to traditional Chinese artifacts, and even fashionable clothes are available. Also, it is quite convenient to get there: just get off at the Ritan stop either by bus or subway.
2. Besides this, Wangfujing Street and Qianmen Street are good places to shop in Beijing. Wangfujing Street is considered No.1 in China, with all kinds of stores. And Qianmen Street is another commercial area, which maintains many branch stores of traditional Chinese brands.
3. If you prefer to get some antiques, the markets at Liulichang and Panjiayuan are recommended.

Key Sentences

1. Is there a department store nearby?

2. Where is the commercial area?

3. Are there 24-hour shops round this neighborhood?

4. Please tell me where I can find an art store in this city.

5. Are there any local product stores?

6. Are there any bargain shops nearby?

7. Are there any shops that sell cameras at affordable prices in this area?

8. Is there a wristwatch shop close by?

9. Are there any discount stores near here?

10. Pardon me. Could you draw a map here?

应用会话 yīng yòng huì huà

1. 这 附 近 有 没 有 百 货 商 店 ？
   Zhè fù jìn yǒu méi yǒu bǎi huò shāng diàn?

2. 商 业 区 在 哪 里 ？
   Shāng yè qū zài nǎ lǐ?

3. 附 近 有 二 十 四 小 时 营 业 的 商 店 吗 ？
   Fù jìn yǒu èr shí sì xiǎo shí yíng yè de shāng diàn ma?

4. 请告诉我这城市里哪儿有工艺品商店。
   Qǐng gào sù wǒ zhè chéng shì lǐ nǎr yǒu gōng yì pǐn shāng diàn.

5. 这 儿 有 卖 土 产 品 的 商 店 吗 ？
   Zhèr yǒu mài tǔ chǎn pǐn de shāng diàn ma?

6. 这 附 近 有 没 有 价 格 便 宜 的 商 店 ？
   Zhè fù jìn yǒu méi yǒu jià gé pián yi de shāng diàn?

7. 这 附 近 有 没 有 卖 照 相 机 便 宜 的 商 店 ？
   Zhè fù jìn yǒu méi yǒu mài zhào xiàng jī pián yi de shāng diàn?

8. 有 专 门 卖 手 表 的 商 店 吗 ？
   Yǒu zhuān mén mài shǒu biǎo de shāng diàn ma?

9. 这 附 近 有 没 有 打 折 的 商 店 ？
   Zhè fù jìn yǒu méi yǒu dǎ zhé de shāng diàn?

10. 麻 烦 您 ，请 在 这 儿 画 一 下 地 图 好 吗 ？
    Má fan nín, qǐng zài zhèr huà yí xià dì tú hǎo ma?

Looking for Shopping Stands

Which floor are the handmade arts and crafts on?

手工艺品在几楼

shǒu gōng yì pǐn zài jǐ lóu

New Words

· pen	钢笔 gāng bǐ	· dress	连衣裙 lián yī qún
· post card	明信片 míng xìn piàn	· stocks	袜子 wà zi
· jacket	上衣 shàng yī	· T-shirt	T恤 T xù
· pants	裤子 kù zi	· underwear	内衣 nèi yī
· skirt	裙子 qún zi	· jeans	牛仔裤 niú zǎi kù
· blouse	女衬衫 nǚ chèn shān	· handkerchief	手帕 shǒu pà

Tips for Trips

1. When you pay bills in shops, usually shop-assistants will give you a ticket which you take to the cashier's desk, and then you can exchange the resulting receipt for the articles you have purchased. Sometimes the shop-assistant will help you with this process.
2. You just have to pass your money and the ticket written out by the shop-assistant to the cashier.
3. Generally, business hours are from 9:00 in the morning to 9:00 in the evening.

Key Sentences

1. Does this shop sell handmade arts and crafts?

2. Where are the electronic products?

3. Which floor is the toyshop on?

4. Where are handmade arts and crafts on display?

5. Welcome! What would you like?

6. I would like to take a look at the rings.

7. Do you have a catalogue of products on discount?

8. Where is the escalator?

9. Where is the elevator?

10. Which floor are clothes for ladies on?

应用会话 yīng yòng huì huà

1. 这 商 店 里 有 手 工 艺 品 卖 吗？
   Zhè shāng diàn lǐ yǒu shǒu gōng yì pǐn mài ma?

2. 电 子 产 品 在 哪 儿？
   Diàn zǐ chǎn pǐn zài nǎr?

3. 玩 具 在 几 楼？
   Wán jù zài jǐ lóu?

4. 手 工 艺 品 在 哪 儿？
   Shǒu gōng yì pǐn zài nǎr ?

5. 欢 迎！ 您 要 什 么？
   Huān yíng! Nín yào shén me?

6. 我 想 看 看 戒 指。
   Wǒ xiǎng kàn kan jiè zhǐ.

7. 有 没 有 降 价 品 介 绍 册？
   Yǒu méi yǒu jiàng jià pǐn jiè shào cè?

8. 电 梯 在 哪 儿？
   Diàn tī zài nǎr?

9. 升 降 梯 在 哪 儿？
   Shēng jiàng tī zài nǎr?

10. 在 几 楼 卖 女 装。
    Zài jǐ lóu mài nǚ zhuāng.

Shopping

Is there anything less expensive?

有没有更便宜的

yǒu méi yǒu gèng pián yi de

New Words

- personal computer 个人电脑 gè rén diàn nǎo
- electronic razor 电动刮脸刀 diàn dòng guā liǎn dāo
- electronic calculator 电子计算机 diàn zǐ jì suàn jī
- recorder 录音机 lù yīn jī
- video camera 录像机 lù xiàng jī
- film camera 电影摄影机 diàn yǐng shè yǐng jī
- lipstick 口红 kǒu hóng
- eyeshade 眼影 yǎn yǐng
- handbag 手提包 shǒu tí bāo
- jewelry 首饰 shǒu shì
- cotton 棉 mián
- silk 丝绸 sī chóu
- woolen knitwear 毛织品 máo zhī pǐn
- leather 皮革 pí gé

1. Big cities in China have an astonishing variety of commodities available. You can buy daily necessities in supermarkets with reasonable prices. Big cities like Beijing have a lot of supermarkets, even Price Smart and SAM Clubs of the USA have branches there.
2. Things sold by some stores located in scenic spots will be relatively expensive. Please be careful when you buy things there. If you really want to buy something, you can ask your Chinese friends to help with bargaining.
3. There are also a lot of small ware wholesale markets and free markets in Beijing, such as Xiushui Street, the Hongqiao Market and the Wantong Small Ware Wholesale Market. In such places you can buy souvenirs with Chinese characteristic, fashionable clothes, or Chinese-style-clothes—Tang clothes. Furthermore, things here are cheaper and prices can be negotiated.

Key Sentences

1. I am only taking a look.

2. I am looking for a CD.

3. Do you have any recorders?

4. Please show me this (that).

5. Can I touch it?

6. Are these all the rings you have ?

7. Do you have them in other styles?

8. Please show me your more (less) expensive ones.

9. Is this pure gold or plated?

10. Is this real?

应用会话 yīng yòng huì huà

1. 我 只 是 看 看 。

   Wǒ zhǐ shì kàn kan.

2. 我 正 在 找 CD 盘 。

   Wǒ zhèng zài zhǎo CD pán.

3. 有 录 音 机 吗 ？

   Yǒu lù yīn jī ma?

4. 请 给 我 看 看 这 个（那 个）。

   Qǐng gěi wǒ kàn kan zhè gè (nà gè).

5. 可 以 摸 一 摸 吗 ？

   Kě yǐ mō yī mō ma?

6. 这 些 是 这 里 的 全 部 戒 指 吗 ？

   Zhè xiē shì zhè lǐ de quán bù jiè zhǐ ma?

7. 有 没 有 别 的 款 式 ？

   Yǒu méi yǒu bié de kuǎn shì?

8. 请 给 我 看 看 更 贵 的（便 宜 的）。

   Qǐng gěi wǒ kàn kan gèng guì de (pián yi de).

9. 这 是 纯 金 的 ， 还 是 镀 金 的 ？

   Zhè shì chún jīn de, hái shì dù jīn de?

10. 这 是 真 的 吗 ？

    Zhè shì zhēn de ma?

Key Sentences

11. What country of origin (brand) is this?

12. Is after-sales service available in France, too?

13. Can you take my measurement?

14. Can I try it on?

15. This material is too flowery (not flowery enough).

16. Do you have anything more (less) flowery?

17. Do you have a larger (smaller) size?

18. It's too big (small). It's too long (short).

19. It is too tight (loose). It fits me well.

20. Can you lower the price a little?

11. 这是哪个国家（牌子）的？
Zhè shì nǎ gè guó jiā (pái zi) de?

12. 在法国也能享受售后服务吗？
Zài Fǎ guó yě néng xiǎng shòu shòu hòu fú wù ma?

13. 请给我量一量尺寸好吗？
Qǐng gěi wǒ liáng yī liáng chǐ cùn hǎo ma?

14. 试穿一下可以吗？
Shì chuān yí xià kě yǐ ma?

15. 这颜色太花（素）。
Zhè yán sè tài huā (sù).

16. 有没有更花（素）的？
Yǒu méi yǒu gèng huā (sù) de?

17. 有没有更大（小）的？
Yǒu méi yǒu gèng dà (xiǎo) de?

18. 太大（小）了。太长（短）了。
Tài dà (xiǎo) le. Tài cháng (duǎn) le.

19. 太紧（松）了。我穿着合身。
Tài jǐn (sōng) le. Wǒ chuān zhe hé shēn.

20. 可以便宜一点吗？
Kě yǐ pián yi yì diǎn ma?

Purchasing and Paying Bills

Do you accept this credit card?

能用这张信用卡吗

néng yòng zhè zhāng xìn yòng kǎ ma

New Words

· how much/ how many	多 少 duō shǎo	· pay	付 钱 fù qián
· gift	礼 物 lǐ wù	· settle the account	算 账 suàn zhàng
· package	包 装 bāo zhuāng	· change	零 钱 líng qián
· ribbon	丝 带 sī dài	· mistake	错 误 cuò wù
· shopping bag	购 物 袋 子 gòu wù dài zi	· mail	投 递 tóu dì
· card	卡 kǎ		
· traveler's check	旅 行 支 票 lǚ xíng zhī piào		

1. As for payment, travelers can use traveler's checks or credit cards, which are mostly accepted in emporiums, supermarkets or hotels.
2. It's better to use RMB when shopping in China, because foreign currency is allowed in just few places.
3. In China, "bargaining" when shopping is common in many places, except in emporiums. If you have a talent in this respect, you can go to China for a try. Remember: if you are not going to buy an item, avoid bargaining. Otherwise, it may cause troubles.

 **Key Sentences**

1. It doesn't appeal to me at all.

2. Excuse me. I want to think it over again.

3. Please give me this (that) then. How much?

4. Please pack them separately.

5. Please put it in a (big) shopping bag.

6. Please take this credit card.

7. Can you send it to the US?

8. I haven't got my change yet.

9. Isn't there a mistake in your account?

10. There is not enough change.

应用会话 yīng yòng huì huà

1. 怎么看也看不上。
Zěn me kàn yě kàn bú shàng.

2. 对不起，我要再想一想。
Duì bu qǐ, wǒ yào zài xiǎng yī xiǎng.

3. 那么请给我这个（那个）。多少钱？
Nà me qǐng gěi wǒ zhè gè (nà gè). Duō shǎo qián?

4. 请分开包装。
Qǐng fēn kāi bāo zhuāng.

5. 请放在（大的）购物袋里面。
Qǐng fàng zài (dà de) gòu wù dài lǐ mian.

6. 请刷这张信用卡。
Qǐng shuā zhè zhāng xìn yòng kǎ.

7. 能不能寄到美国？
Néng bù néng jì dào Měi guó?

8. 还没找回零钱。
Hái méi zhǎo huí líng qián.

9. 是不是算错账了？
Shì bú shì suàn cuò zhàng le?

10. 零钱不够。
Líng qián bú gòu.

Looking for Tour Buses

When does the bus leave?
汽车几点出发
qì chē jǐ diǎn chū fā

New Words

- travel agency 旅游代理店 lǚ yóu dài lǐ diàn
- travel service 旅行社 lǚ xíng shè
- one-day tour guide 一天导游 yì tiān dǎo yóu
- half-day tour guide 半天导游 bàn tiān dǎo yóu
- nighttime tour guide 夜间导游 yè jiān dǎo yóu
- tour 游览 yóu lǎn
- explanation 说明 shuō míng
- tour guide 导游 dǎo yóu
- interpreter 翻译 fān yì
- map 地图 dì tú
- leaflet 小册子 xiǎo cè zi

Tips for Trips

1. By applying for one-day excursion you can have a whole day's or a half day's wonderful experience.
2. If you want to apply for your favorite one day excursion, you can consult the China International Travel Service (CITS). Their service line in Beijing is:010-66011122

Key Sentences

1. Where is the travel agency?

2. Please give me a travel service manual.

3. How many types of tour guides do you offer?

4. Do you have any city tour guides?

5. Are there any English (French) speaking tour guides?

6. When and where do we depart?

7. When will we get back?

8. What's the total cost for this (that) travel line?

9. Can we make reservations here?

10. What additional costs are there?

应用会话 yīng yòng huì huà

1. 旅行社在哪儿？
   Lǚ xíng shè zài nǎr?

2. 请给我旅游服务手册。
   Qǐng gěi wǒ lǚ yóu fú wù shǒu cè.

3. 导游有多少种？
   Dǎo yóu yǒu duō shǎo zhǒng?

4. 有市区导游吗？
   Yǒu shì qū dǎo yóu ma?

5. 有没有说英语（法语）的导游？
   Yǒu méi yǒu shuō Yīng yǔ (Fǎ yǔ) de dǎo yóu?

6. 在哪儿几点出发？
   Zài nǎr jǐ diǎn chū fā?

7. 什么时候能回来？
   Shén me shí hòu néng huí lái?

8. 这（那）条旅游线路多少钱？
   Zhè (nà) tiáo lǚ yóu xiàn lù duō shǎo qián?

9. 可以在这儿预订吗？
   Kě yǐ zài zhèr yù dìng ma?

10. 不包括的费用是什么费用？
    Bù bāo kuò de fèi yòng shì shén me fèi yòng?

Visiting Art Galleries and Museums

How much is a child ticket?

小孩儿票多少钱

xiǎo háir piào duō shǎo qián

New Words

English	Chinese	English	Chinese
museum	博物馆 bó wù guǎn	painting	画 huà
art gallery	美术馆 měi shù guǎn	sculpture	雕刻 diāo kè
introduction leaflet	介绍手册 jiè shào shǒu cè	works	作品 zuò pǐn
display	展示 zhǎn shì	author	作者 zuò zhě
adult	大人 dà rén	close the door	关门 guān mén
child	小孩子 xiǎo hái zi	entrance ticket	门票 mén piào

1. China has countless scenic spots and historic sites.
2. Please note that photography is forbidden in some specific places.
3. Introductions to scenic spots and historic sites have been compiled in this book; please refer to Part IV—Famous Tourist Sites in China.

Key Sentences

1. Is it open now?

2. When will it be open for visitors?

3. When do you close?

4. Are there any English (French) introduction leaflets?

5. How much is a (child) ticket?

6. What is this?

7. Marvelous!

8. When was this work produced?

9. Who is this artist?

10. Is photography forbidden here?

应用会话 yīng yòng huì huà

1. 现 在 可 以 开 始 参 观 吗 ？

   Xiàn zài kě yǐ kāi shǐ cān guān ma?

2. 等 多 长 时 间 才 能 参 观 ？

   Děng duō cháng shí jiān cái néng cān guān?

3. 几 点 关 门 ？

   Jǐ diǎn guān mén?

4. 有 英 文（法 文）介 绍 手 册 吗 ？

   Yǒu Yīng wén (Fǎ wén) jiè shào shǒu cè ma?

5. （小 孩 子）票 价 多 少 钱 ？

   (Xiǎo hái zi) piào jià duō shǎo qián?

6. 这 个 是 什 么 ？

   Zhè gè shì shén me?

7. 好 极 了 ！

   Hǎo jí le!

8. 是 什 么 时 代 的 作 品 ？

   Shì shén me shí dài de zuò pǐn?

9. 这 位 作 者 是 谁 ？

   Zhè wèi zuò zhě shì shéi?

10. 这 里 是 禁 止 拍 摄 的 地 方 吗 ？

    Zhè lǐ shì jìn zhǐ pāi shè de dì fāng ma?

Sightseeing

Marvelous!

好极了

hǎo jí le

New Words

· famous spots and ancient sites	名 胜 古 迹 míng shèng gǔ jì	· lake	湖 hú
· historical sites	史 迹 shǐ jì	· sea	大 海 dà hǎi
· relics	遗 迹 yí jì	· seaside	海 边 hǎi biān
· city wall	城 墙 chéng qiáng	· waterfall	瀑 布 pù bù
· temple	寺 院 sì yuàn	· scenery	景 致 jǐng zhì
· courtyard	庭 院 tíng yuàn	· hot spring	温 泉 wēn quán
· botanical garden	植 物 园 zhí wù yuán	· local product shop	土 产 商 店 tǔ chǎn shāng diàn
· aquarium	水 族 馆 shuǐ zú guǎn		

Tips for Trips

1. Before you begin your visit, in order to increase your appreciation, you can read relevant introductions about the scenic spots and historic sites, and can also ask the professional guide on the spot to show you around.
2. As there may be many people visiting, please take good care of your articles.

Key Sentences

1. Please introduce to us some local sightseeing spots.

2. Let's meet here two hours from now.

3. When was this building built?

4. What's this (that)?

5. One moment please. I need to use the toilet.

6. Where can we take a sightseeing boat (funicular railway)?

7. Is there a coffee shop (restaurant) nearby?

8. Where is there a local crafts shop?

9. When will the bus arrive?

10. What time do we meet?

应用会话 yīng yòng huì huà

1. 请介绍一下这里值得游览的地方。
   Qǐng jiè shào yí xià zhè lǐ zhí dé yóu lǎn de dì fang.

2. 两个小时后在这儿见吧。
   Liǎng gè xiǎo shí hòu zài zhèr jiàn ba.

3. 这个建筑物是什么时代的？
   Zhè gè jiàn zhù wù shì shén me shí dài de?

4. 这个（那个）是什么？
   Zhè gè (nà gè) shì shén me?

5. 请等一下，我要去卫生间。
   Qǐng děng yí xià, wǒ yào qù wèi shēng jiān.

6. 坐游船（缆车）的地方在哪儿？
   Zuò yóu chuán (lǎn chē) de dì fāng zài nǎr?

7. 这附近有没有咖啡厅（餐厅）？
   Zhè fù jìn yǒu méi yǒu kā fēi tīng (cān tīng)?

8. 土产商店在哪儿？
   Tǔ chǎn shāng diàn zài nǎr?

9. 汽车什么时候到？
   Qì chē shén me shí hou dào?

10. 几点集合？
    Jǐ diǎn jí hé?

Taking Photos

Excuse me. Can you help me take a photograph?

麻烦你，能给照张相吗

má fan nǐ, néng gěi zhào zhāng xiàng ma

New Words

· photograph	照片 zhào piàn	· souvenir picture	纪念照 jì niàn zhào
· take a picture	照相 zhào xiàng	· color film	彩色胶卷 cǎi sè jiāo juǎn
· shutter	快门 kuài mén	· B/W film	黑白胶卷 hēi bái jiāo juǎn
· together	一起 yì qǐ	· 24-piece film	二十四张胶卷 èr shí sì zhāng jiāo juǎn
· battery	电池 diàn chí	· No photography	禁止拍照 jìn zhǐ pāi zhào
· film developing	冲洗 chōng xǐ	· No flash photography	禁止用闪光灯 jìn zhǐ yòng shǎn guāng dēng

1. Please don't take many things with you wherever you go.
2. It's wise to bring along your camera. Nowadays young people in China prefer digital cameras.
3. Color film: about ¥20 /(36 pieces) about ¥14/(24 pieces)
   Black-and-white film: about ¥7/(36 pieces) about ¥4 /(24 pieces)

Key Sentences

1. Can I take a picture here?

2. Can I use the flashlight?

3. Is photography forbidden here (in the museum)?

4. Please just press here. Thank you.

5. Excuse us. Please take another one for us.

6. Do you mind taking a picture with me?

7. Can I take a picture of you?

8. I would like to send this picture to you. Could you write down your name and address here?

9. Please give me a 24-piece color film.

10. I would like a B/W film.

应用会话 yīng yòng huì huà

1. 可以在这里照相吗？
   Kě yǐ zài zhè lǐ zhào xiàng ma?

2. 可以使用闪光灯吗？
   Kě yǐ shǐ yòng shǎn guāng dēng ma?

3. 禁止在这里（馆内）照相吗？
   Jìn zhǐ zài zhè lǐ (guǎn nèi) zhào xiàng ma?

4. 请按这儿就行。
   Qǐng àn zhèr jiù xíng.

5. 对不起，请再给照一张。
   Duì bu qǐ, qǐng zài gěi zhào yì zhāng.

6. 不介意的话，一起照张相好吗？
   Bú jiè yì de huà, yì qǐ zhào zhāng xiàng hǎo ma?

7. 可以照你的相吗？
   Kě yǐ zhào nǐ de xiàng ma?

8. 照片寄给你，请把姓名和地址写在这儿好吗？
   Zhào piàn jì gěi nǐ, qǐng bǎ xìng míng hé dì zhǐ xiě zài zhèr hǎo ma?

9. 请给我二十四张的彩色胶卷。
   Qǐng gěi wǒ èr shí sì zhāng de cǎi sè jiāo juǎn.

10. 我要买黑白胶卷。
    Wǒ yào mǎi hēi bái jiāo juǎn.

Watching Operas, Movies and Shows

I fancy traditional art.

我想看传统艺术

wǒ xiǎng kàn chuán tǒng yì shù

New Words

- traditional art 传统艺术 chuán tǒng yì shù
- Chinese dance 中国舞蹈 zhōng guó wǔ dǎo
- music drama 音乐剧 yīn yuè jù
- ballet 芭蕾舞 bā lěi wǔ
- cinema 电影院 diàn yǐng yuàn
- theatre 剧场 jù chǎng
- hero 主角 zhǔ jué
- play the part of 出演 chū yǎn
- director 导演 dǎo yǎn
- conductor 指挥 zhǐ huī
- performance 演奏 yǎn zòu
- entrance ticket 门票 mén piào
- sold out 卖光了 mài guāng le

1. Beijing opera is a kind of traditional arts cherished by Chinese people. It is famous for the players' peculiar movements, magnificent dresses, unique face-paintings and characteristic voice performances.
2. In ancient times, Beijing opera was only performed by males. But in modern times there are women players too.
3. Acrobatics is also a kind of traditional Chinese arts. Wuqiao town in Hebei Province is recognized as the "town of acrobatics". Each year the "Acrobatics Art Festival" is held there.

Key Sentences

1. I fancy traditional art (Chinese film).

2. Is there a service desk?

3. Can reservations be made here?

4. Where can I get a ticket?

5. Where will it be performed?

6. What performance is being put on ?

7. When does it begin?

8. When does it end?

9. What hour will the next performance be performed?

10. Where is this seat?

应用会话 yīng yòng huì huà

1. 我 想 看 传 统 艺 术（中 国 电 影）。
   Wǒ xiǎng kàn chuán tǒng yì shù (zhōng guó diàn yǐng).

2. 有 服 务 台 吗？
   Yǒu fú wù tái ma?

3. 在 这 儿 可 以 预 订 吗？
   Zài zhèr kě yǐ yù dìng ma?

4. 在 哪 儿 买 票？
   Zài nǎr mǎi piào?

5. 在 哪 儿 上 演？
   Zài nǎr shàng yǎn?

6. 正 在 上 演 的 节 目 是 什 么？
   Zhèng zài shàng yǎn de jié mù shì shén me?

7. 几 点 开 始？
   Jǐ diǎn kāi shǐ?

8. 几 点 结 束？
   Jǐ diǎn jié shù?

9. 下 个 节 目 几 点 上 演？
   Xià gè jié mù jǐ diǎn shàng yǎn?

10. 这 个 座 位 在 哪 儿？
    Zhè gè zuò wèi zài nǎr?

Going to Bars and Discos

Please tell me which hotel offers cheap and tasty wine.

请告诉我哪儿的酒店酒又好喝又便宜

qǐng gào su wǒ nǎr de jiǔ diàn jiǔ yòu hǎo hē yòu pián yi

New Words

- disco 迪斯科 dí sī kē
- nightclub 夜总会 yè zǒng huì
- bar 酒吧 jiǔ bā
- restaurant 酒家 jiǔ jiā
- karaoke 卡拉 OK kǎ lā OK
- beer 啤酒 pí jiǔ
- maotai 茅台酒 máo tái jiǔ
- spirit 烧酒 shāo jiǔ
- whisky 威士忌 wēi shì jì
- cocktail 鸡尾酒 jī wěi jiǔ
- dishes to go with wine 酒菜 jiǔ cài

Tips for Trips

1. Though there are not any pubs in China, drink is consumable in restaurants of all sizes. Big cities also have a lot of special bar streets, which have both styles that westerners are familiar with and styles with Chinese characteristic. You can go to bars in the evening after a day of travel, perhaps you may run into your own compatriots there.
2. The "San Li Tun" bars in Beijing are very famous. They lie in the east district of Beijing, adjoining the embassy district. If you go there by taxi, few taxi drivers in Beijing don't know the place.
3. Bigger cities in China may have clubs, and some bars will provide their customers with dancing music too.

Key Sentences

1. What's the most well-known dancing hall in Beijing?

2. How much is the cover charge?

3. Are drinks (meals) not included?

4. Do you mind dancing with me?

5. Is there a nightclub (bar) in this hotel?

6. Please show me your price list.

7. Do you have a menu with pictures?

8. Please bring us this, this, and this.

9. What dish is this?

10. Please let me have two bottles of beer (zhuyeqing liquor).

应用会话 yīng yòng huì huà

1. 北京最有名的舞厅在哪儿？
   Běi jīng zuì yǒu míng de wǔ tīng zài nǎr?

2. 门票多少钱？
   Mén piào duō shǎo qián?

3. 不包括饮料费（餐费）吗？
   Bù bāo kuò yǐn liào fèi (cān fèi) ma?

4. 不介意的话，一起跳个舞好吗？
   Bú jiè yì de huà, yì qǐ tiào gè wǔ hǎo ma?

5. 这饭店里有夜总会（酒吧）吗？
   Zhè fàn diàn lǐ yǒu yè zǒng huì (jiǔ bā) ma?

6. 请给我看一看价格单。
   Qǐng gěi wǒ kàn yī kàn jià gé dān.

7. 有没有带照片的菜单？
   Yǒu méi yǒu dài zhào piàn de cài dān?

8. 请给我这个、那个和那个。
   Qǐng gěi wǒ zhè gè, nà gè hé nà gè.

9. 这是什么菜？
   Zhè shì shén me cài?

10. 请给我两瓶啤酒（竹叶青酒）。
    Qǐng gěi wǒ liǎng píng pí jiǔ (zhú yè qīng jiǔ).

Swimming Pool, Tennis Court and Golf Course

How much do you charge for your golf course?

网球场1小时多少钱

wǎng qiú chǎng yì xiǎo shí duō shǎo qián

New Words

- swimming pool 游泳池 yóu yǒng chí
- golf course 高尔夫球场 gāo ěr fū qiú chǎng
- tennis court 网球场 wǎng qiú chǎng
- ride a bicycle 骑自行车 qí zì xíng chē
- swimming suit 游泳衣 yóu yǒng yī
- tennis shoes 网球鞋 wǎng qiú xié
- golf club 高尔夫球俱乐部 gāo ěr fū qiú jù lè bù
- racket 拍子 pāi zi
- ski 滑雪 huá xuě
- skate 溜冰 liū bīng
- swim 游泳 yóu yǒng
- climb the mountain 爬山 pá shān
- fish 钓鱼 diào yú
- ride a horse 骑马 qí mǎ

Tips for Trips

1. There are a lot of bowling halls, tennis courts and golf courses in China. In hotels above the middle-grade, you can enjoy these recreational facilities with a little money.
2. People who are staying in hotels are charged differently from people who aren't.

Category	Non Hotel Guests	Hotel Guests
Swimming pool	¥50	Free
Tennis	¥100/per hour (differs from hotels)	
Golf	¥975 (one game /18 caves)	

Key Sentences

1. Is there a swimming pool in this hotel?

2. Are there charges for using the swimming pool?

3. What are the costs for using your fitness club?

4. Do you rent tennis racket?

5. Is there a golf course nearby?

6. Can reservations be made here?

7. Is it far from here?

8. How do I get there from here?

9. Besides this, what other sports equipment is there?

10. Are they open for use 24 hours a day?

应用会话 yīng yòng huì huà

1. 这 家 饭 店 里 有 游 泳 池 吗 ？
   Zhè jiā fàn diàn lǐ yǒu yóu yǒng chí ma?

2. 游 泳 要 给 钱 吗 ？
   Yóu yǒng yào gěi qián ma?

3. 使 用 健 身 俱 乐 部 的 费 用 是 多 少 钱 ？
   Shǐ yòng jiàn shēn jù lè bù de fèi yòng shì duō shǎo qián?

4. 可 以 租 网 球 拍 吗 ？
   Kě yǐ zū wǎng qiú pāi ma?

5. 这 附 近 能 打 高 尔 夫 球 吗 ？
   Zhè fù jìn néng dǎ gāo ěr fū qiú ma?

6. 在 这 儿 可 以 预 订 吗 ？
   Zài zhèr kě yǐ yù dìng ma?

7. 那 个 地 方 离 这 儿 近 吗 ？
   Nà gè dì fang lí zhèr jìn ma?

8. 到 那 个 地 方 从 这 儿 怎 么 走 ？
   Dào nà gè dì fang cóng zhèr zěn me zǒu?

9. 另 外 ， 还 有 些 什 么 体 育 设 施 ？
   Lìng wài, hái yǒu xiē shén me tǐ yù shè shī?

10. 可 以 二 十 四 小 时 使 用 吗 ？
    Kě yǐ èr shí sì xiǎo shí shǐ yòng ma?

Visiting a Chinese Family

Excuse me.

麻烦您

má fan nín

New Words

· visit	访 问 fǎng wèn	· wife or husband	爱 人 ài rén
· invite	邀 请 yāo qǐng	· husband	丈 夫 zhàng fū
· gift	礼 物 lǐ wù	· child	孩 子 hái zi
· tea	茶 chá	· our	我 们 的 wǒ men de
· nothing special	没什么特别的 méi shén me tè bié de	· your	您 的 nín de

Tips for Trips

1. Chinese people seldom invite guests to their houses except for good friends. Once they have invited friends to their homes, they will serve them very warmly.
2. When you are invited, you'd better take a small present. If the visit is prearranged, getting the presents ready ahead of time can save you many inconveniences.
3. Generally, you can say "hello" as a greeting. As a reference, please note that Chinese people have the habits of repeating "hello".

Key Sentences

1. Thank you for your invitation.

2. It is an insignificant gift. Please accept it.

3. The house (decoration) looks very pretty.

4. What dish is this? It's very delicious.

5. Very good tea.

6. I've had a pleasant day.

7. Please visit us at our home when you come to the US.

8. I've determined to study Chinese hard after I get back home.

9. I'll write to you immediately after I get back to the US.

10. We'll leave now. Please don't bother to see us off.

应用会话 yīng yòng huì huà

1. 谢 谢 您 的 邀 请 。
   Xiè xie nín de yāo qǐng.

2. 是 小 小 的 礼 物 ，请 收 下 。
   Shì xiǎo xiǎo de lǐ wù, qǐng shōu xià.

3. 房 子 （ 装 饰 品 ）很 好 看 。
   Fáng zi (zhuāng shì pǐn) hěn hǎo kàn.

4. 这 是 什 么 菜 ？ 很 好 吃 。
   Zhè shì shén me cài? Hěn hǎo chī.

5. 茶 很 好 喝 。
   Chá hěn hǎo hē.

6. 今 天 过 得 很 愉 快 。
   Jīn tiān guò de hěn yú kuài.

7. 以 后 您 来 美 国 时 ，请 到 我 家 来 做 客 。
   Yǐ hòu nín lái Měi guó shí, qǐng dào wǒ jiā lái zuò kè.

8. 回 国 以 后 我 一 定 好 好 学 习 中 文 。
   Huí guó yǐ hòu wǒ yí dìng hǎo hǎo xué xí Zhōng wén.

9. 回 美 国 以 后 ，就 马 上 给 您 写 信 。
   Huí Měi guó yǐ hòu, jiù mǎ shàng gěi nín xiě xìn.

10. 要 走 了 ，请 留 步 。
    Yào zǒu le, qǐng liú bù.

Making Domestic Phone Calls

Hi, it's me. Do you remember?

喂，是我，还记得吗

wèi, shì wǒ, hái jì de ma

New Words

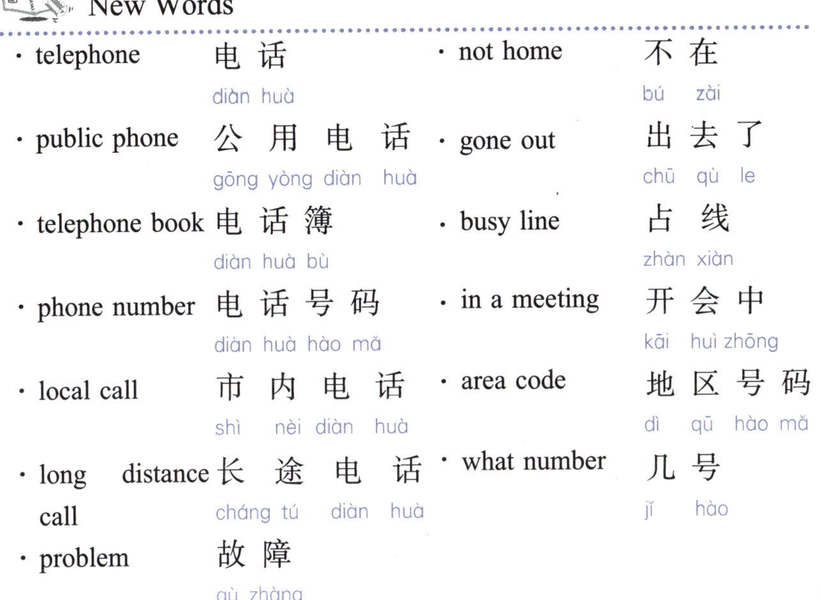

English	Chinese	Pinyin	English	Chinese	Pinyin
telephone	电话	diàn huà	not home	不在	bú zài
public phone	公用电话	gōng yòng diàn huà	gone out	出去了	chū qù le
telephone book	电话簿	diàn huà bù	busy line	占线	zhàn xiàn
phone number	电话号码	diàn huà hào mǎ	in a meeting	开会中	kāi huì zhōng
local call	市内电话	shì nèi diàn huà	area code	地区号码	dì qū hào mǎ
long distance call	长途电话	cháng tú diàn huà	what number	几号	jǐ hào
problem	故障	gù zhàng			

Tips for Trips

1. Please add the area code before the numbers you want to dial.
2. Usually the "public telephones" in streets can only be used for local calls and domestic long-distance calls. The charge standard of local calls is three ~five *mao* per minute, namely, less than 5 cents per minute.

P.S: *Mao* is equal to one tenth of *yuan*.

Key Sentences

1. Hi. This is Martin. Is Mr. Wang in?

2. Who is speaking please?

3. One moment please.

4. Mr. Wang is not in.

5. What time will he be back?

6. Please ask him to call me back after he returns.

7. My number is 61234567.

8. I 'm in Room 108 of the Beijing Hotel.

9. Sorry. I dialed the wrong number.

10. Where is there a public phone?

应用会话 yīng yòng huì huà

1. 喂，我是马丁，王先生在吗？
   Wèi, wǒ shì Mǎ dīng, Wáng xiān sheng zài ma?

2. 您是哪一位？
   Nín shì nǎ yí wèi?

3. 请等一下。
   Qǐng děng yí xià.

4. 王先生现在不在。
   Wáng xiān sheng xiàn zài bú zài.

5. 几点回来呢？
   Jǐ diǎn huí lái ne?

6. 他回来后，请转告他给我打个电话。
   Tā huí lái hòu, qǐng zhuǎn gào tā gěi wǒ dǎ gè diàn huà.

7. 电话号码是6123-4567。
   Diàn huà hào mǎ shì liù yī èr sān-sì wǔ liù qī.

8. 我住在北京饭店108号房间。
   Wǒ zhù zài Běi jīng Fàn diàn yī líng bā hào fáng jiān.

9. 对不起，打错了。
   Duì bu qǐ, dǎ cuò le.

10. 公用电话在哪儿？
    Gōng yòng diàn huà zài nǎr?

Making International Phone Calls

I want to make an international long distance call.

我要打国际电话

wǒ yào dǎ guó jì diàn huà

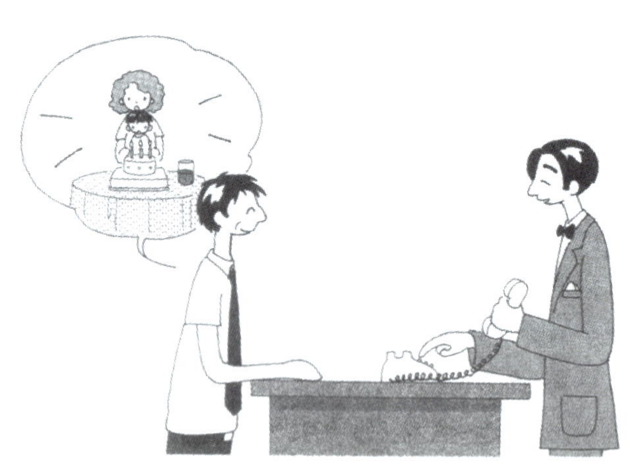

New Words

- international call 国际电话 guó jì diàn huà
- aided call 叫人电话 jiào rén diàn huà
- collect call 对方付钱 duì fāng fù qián
- country code 国家号码 guó jiā hào mǎ

Tips for Trips

1. Making international phone calls

   When making international phone calls, first dial "00"—the international calling code, then the country code, then the area code (when the first number of the area code is "0", please leave it out), last dial the telephone numbers you want.

2. Phone cards are sold in most big and medium cities of China, and the price usually will not exceed the value on the card's face. Sometimes, at small stands by the street you can buy cards at a price lower than their card value. There are three kinds of card, ¥30, ¥50 and ¥100. More conveniently, there are many telephone booths and operator-run telephone stores in the big and medium cities of China.

Key Sentences

1. I want to place an international call to London, England.

2. Please tell me your name and room number.

3. I'm Smith and my room number is 231.

4. What's the number you are calling?

5. It's 0044-2078123456 in London.

6. Mr. Wang please.

7. Your line is through. Please speak.

8. The line is busy. /Nobody is answering the phone.

9. Can I call international long distance with this public phone?

10. Please speak slowly.

应用会话 yīng yòng huì huà

1. 我 要 往 英 国 的 伦 敦 打 国 际 电 话 。
Wǒ yào wǎng Yīng guó de Lún dūn dǎ guó jì diàn huà.

2. 请 告 诉 我 您 的 姓 名 和 房 间 号 码 。
Qǐng gào sù wǒ nín de xìng míng hé fáng jiān hào mǎ.

3. 我 是 史 密 斯 ，231 号 房 间 。
Wǒ shì Shǐ mì sī, èr sān yī hào fáng jiān.

4. 对 方 的 电 话 号 码 是 几 号 ？
Duì fāng de diàn huà hào mǎ shì jǐ hào?

5. 伦 敦 0044-2078123456 。
Lún dūn líng líng sì sì–èr líng qī bā yī èr sān sì wǔ liù.

6. 找 王 先 生 。
Zhǎo Wáng xiān sheng.

7. 接 通 了 ，请 讲 话 。
Jiē tōng le, Qǐng jiǎng huà.

8. 占 线 。/ 没 人 接 。
Zhàn xiàn. /Méi rén jiē.

9. 用 这 个 公 用 电 话 可 以 打 国 际 电 话 吗 ？
Yòng zhè gè gōng yòng diàn huà kě yǐ dǎ guó jì diàn huà ma?

10. 请 慢 点 说 。
Qǐng màn diǎn shuō.

At the Post office

Please post it by sea.

请用海运寄

qǐng yòng hǎi yùn jì

New Words

- post office 邮局 yóu jú
- writing paper 信纸 xìn zhǐ
- envelope 信封 xìn fēng
- stamp 邮票 yóu piào
- postcard 明信片 míng xìn piàn
- address 地址 dì zhǐ
- postal code 邮政编码 yóu zhèng biān mǎ
- sender 寄信人 jì xìn rén
- receiver 收信人 shōu xìn rén

The logo of China Post is green. If you want to know more about China Post, please visit the website at:
http://www.chinapost.gov.cn/English/index.htm

International Postal Rate of China Post

Currency Unit: RMB¥

Category	Weight	Rate Standard
Letters	20 grams and below	4.40
	20 to 50 grams	8.20
	50 to 100 grams	10.40
	100 to 250 grams	20.80
	250 to 500 grams	39.80
	500 to 1000 grams	75.70
	1000 to 2000 grams	123.00
Postcard	Each	3.20
Airmail	Each	5.20
Packages	100 grams and below	7.80
	100 to 250 grams	15.70
	250 to 500 grams	28.30
	500 to 1000 grams	46.90
	1000 to 2000 grams	87.80

Post offices of China basically open throughout the whole year. Business hours of the post offices in Beijing are generally from 8:00 a.m. to 6:30 p.m..

Zip codes of major cities in China:

Beijing:100000

Shanghai:200000

Tianjin 300000

Chongqing:400000
Guangzhou:510000
Nanjing:210000
Hangzhou 310000
Kunming 650000
Jinan 250000
Fuzhou:350000

Services provided by Express Mail Service(EMS) across China are as follows:

Mailing delivery service at post offices:

You can take the letter or parcel you need to send to a nearby post office.

On-site service:

In response to your call to the on-site service number 185, the post office will collect and deliver the mail on site.

Acting as a customshouse agent:

Going through customs declaration procedures on behalf of the customers for their mails or goods (samples).

Packing service for customers:

While delivering mails with EMS, post offices will offer packing boxes of various sizes and do the packing for you.

International & domestic cargo-transportation service:

Transportation services by air and by sea are provided for international and domestic cargoes, including the entire process of exports-transfer from production sites to shipping destinations and imports-transfer from harbors to consignors.

Gift delivery service:

Postal gift delivery service can deliver fresh flowers, cakes, congratulation cards and invitations for you.

Local special delivery service:

In case of urgent letters and parcels, post offices will send specific staff and vehicle for the delivery within limited time.

Tracking & inquiry service:

Adopting an advanced computer inquiry system, EMS provides tracking & inquiry service for your express mails.

Key Sentences

1. Where is the post office?

2. Is there a mailbox nearby?

3. I want to send this letter (parcel) to France.

4. Please post it by air (sea).

5. Please send it express mail (registered).

6. How much is it by air (sea/express mail/registered)?

7. Where are stamps sold?

8. Please let me have a three-yuan stamp.

9. Where is the EMS window?

10. Please give me five postcards.

应用会话 yīng yòng huì huà

1. 邮局在哪儿？
   Yóu jú zài nǎr?

2. 这附近有信箱吗？
   Zhè fù jìn yǒu xìn xiāng ma?

3. 我想把这封信（包裹）寄到法国。
   Wǒ xiǎng bǎ zhè fēng xìn (bāo guǒ) jì dào Fǎ guó.

4. 请用航空（海运）寄去。
   Qǐng yòng háng kōng (hǎi yùn) jì qù.

5. 请寄快递信（挂号信）。
   Qǐng jì kuài dì xìn (guà hào xìn).

6. 用航空（海运、快递信、挂号信）多少钱？
   Yòng háng kōng (hǎi yùn, kuài dì xìn, guà hào xìn) duō shǎo qián?

7. 在哪儿卖邮票？
   Zài nǎr mài yóu piào?

8. 请给我3元的邮票。
   Qǐng gěi wǒ sān yuán de yóu piào.

9. EMS窗口在哪儿？
   EMS chuāng kǒu zài nǎr?

10. 请给我5张明信片。
    Qǐng gěi wǒ wǔ zhāng míng xìn piàn.

At the Bank

Please convert it into RMB.

请 换 成 人 民 币

qǐng huàn chéng Rén mín bì

New Words

- bank 银行 yín háng
- coin 硬币 yìng bì
- bank note 钞票 chāo piào
- check 支票 zhī piào
- draft 汇票 huì piào
- cash 现金 xiàn jīn
- change money 换钱 huàn qián
- yuan 元 yuán
- window 窗口 chuāng kǒu
- paper 用纸 yòng zhǐ
- fill in 填写 tián xiě
- headquarters 总店 zǒng diàn
- branch 分店 fēn diàn

1. Generally banks in China are run by the state, such as the Bank of China, the Industrial and Commercial Bank of China, the Construction Bank of China, the Agriculture Bank of China, etc.
2. Chinese citizens, as well as foreigners living in China, can open their own bank accounts, or visa cards.
3. Only workers living permanently in the local city can apply for a credit card.

Key Sentences

1. Is there a bank close by?

2. Please cash this traveler's check.

3. I want five one-hundred and five fifty notes.

4. Here is 2000 yuan, would you please change it into smaller bills?

5. Where is the foreign currency bank of the Beijing branch?

6. May I please ask how to go to the foreign exchange bank?

7. I want to change some money into RMB. Which window is it?

8. I want to convert all these to RMB.

9. How much is the exchange rate for RMB today?

10. Do you convert from currencies other than US dollars?

应用会话 yīng yòng huì huà

1. 这附近有银行吗？
Zhè fù jìn yǒu yín háng ma?

2. 请把旅行支票换成现金。
Qǐng bǎ lǚ xíng zhī piào huàn chéng xiàn jīn.

3. 我要5张一百元的、5张五十元的。
Wǒ yào wǔ zhāng yì bǎi yuán de, wǔ zhāng wǔ shí yuán de.

4. 请把这两千元帮我破开。
Qǐng bǎ zhè liǎng qiān yuán bāng wǒ pò kāi.

5. 北京分行的外换银行在哪儿？
Běi jīng fēn háng de wài huàn yín háng zài nǎr?

6. 请问一下，到外换银行怎么走？
Qǐng wèn yí xià, dào wài huàn yín háng zěn me zǒu?

7. 我要换人民币，窗口在哪儿？
Wǒ yào huàn Rén mín bì, chuāng kǒu zài nǎr?

8. 我要把这些全部换成人民币。
Wǒ yào bǎ zhè xiē quán bù huàn chéng Rén mín bì.

9. 今天兑人民币的汇率是多少？
Jīn tiān duì Rén mín bì de huì lǜ shì duō shǎo?

10. 除美金以外的货币也可换吗？
Chú Měi jīn yǐ wài de huò bì yě kě huàn ma?

Getting Lost

May I please ask where the Beijing Hotel is?

请问，北京饭店在哪儿

qǐng wèn , Běi jīng Fàn diàn zài nǎr

New Words

- way 路 lù
- map 地图 dì tú
- enquiry 询问 xún wèn
- direction 方向 fāng xiàng
- where 哪儿 nǎr
- English 英语 Yīng yǔ
- Chinese characters 汉字 hàn zì
- station house 派出所 pài chū suǒ
- station 站 zhàn
- building 建筑物 jiàn zhù wù
- right 右边 yòu bian
- left 左边 zuǒ bian

Tips for Trips

1. Ask the police for help when you've become lost, as the Chinese saying goes, "When you meet difficulties, ask the police for help."
2. You'd better take a map and the telephone number of the place you're staying with you when you go out.
3. Use the following expressions when getting lost:
   - "对不起,到××饭店怎么走?" (Duì bu qǐ, dào ×× fàndiàn zěnme zǒu?) Excuse me, can you tell me how to get to the ... hotel?
   - "请告诉我,到××饭店该怎么走?"(Qǐng gàosu wǒ, dào ×× fàndiàn gāi zěnme zǒu?) Please tell me the way to ... hotel.

Key Sentences

1. Could you tell me if there is a station house nearby?

2. I've lost my way. Where is the Beijing Hotel?

3. I am a tourist from Canada.

4. May I bother you to write in English on my map?

5. Excuse me. Could you take me there?

6. Pardon me. Is this the way to the Beijing Railway Station?

7. Will this take me to the Beijing Railway Station?

8. Thank you for helping me .

9. Which is the right way?

10. Is it a long way on foot?

应用会话 yīng yòng huì huà

1. 请问，这附近有没有派出所？
Qǐng wèn, zhè fù jìn yǒu méi yǒu pài chū suǒ?

2. 我迷路了，北京饭店在哪儿？
Wǒ mí lù le, Běi jīng Fàn diàn zài nǎr?

3. 我是从加拿大来的游客。
Wǒ shì cóng Jiā ná dà lái de yóu kè.

4. 麻烦您，请在地图上标记英文。
Má fan nín, qǐng zài dì tú shàng biāo jì Yīng wén.

5. 麻烦您，带我去那儿附近好吗？
Má fan nín, dài wǒ qù nàr fù jìn hǎo ma?

6. 请问一下，去北京站走这个方向对吗？
Qǐng wèn yí xià, qù Běi jīng zhàn zǒu zhè gè fāng xiàng duì ma?

7. 走这条路可以到北京站吗？
Zǒu zhè tiáo lù kě yǐ dào Běi jīng zhàn ma?

8. 谢谢帮我的忙。
Xiè xie bāng wǒ de máng.

9. 走哪个方向是对的呢？
Zǒu nǎ gè fāng xiàng shì duì de ne?

10. 走着远吗？
Zǒu zhe yuǎn ma?

Losing Things

I lost my passport.

我丢了护照

wǒ diū le hù zhào

New Words

· lose	遗失 yí shī	· where	在哪儿 zài nǎr
· passport	护照 hù zhào	· taxi	出租汽车 chū zū qì chē
· purse	钱包 qián bāo	· contact	联系 lián xì
· handbag	手提包 shǒu tí bāo	· lost & found office	遗失品保管所 yí shī pǐn bǎo guǎn suǒ
· traveler's check	旅行支票 lǚ xíng zhī piào	· lost & found registration	遗失品申报 yí shī pǐn shēn bào

Tips for Trips

- Loss of property

As soon as you lose money or other property in Beijing, report the loss to the entry and exit administrative department of the local police station at the place where you lost your property and answer the relevant questions. The following procedures need to be carried out:

Hand in your passport and valid ID for a check.

Fill in the "Explanation of the Loss". Try to include details such as time, location, the process, a description and the value of the lost property.

If traveler's checks or credit cards are lost, you should report the loss to the police as well as to bank immediately.

Please leave your temporary address or your permanent address, your telephone number, the contact person, and also your address in your own country and the postal code, so that the police can contact you as soon as they find your articles.

- Losing your passport in China

If you lose your passport in China, you have to report the loss to the entry and exit administrative department of the police station immediately, indicating the time and the location, the process, the passport number and its expiration date. The owner of the lost property, after having declared and received "proof of reporting the loss of passport", should go to their own country's embassy in China to apply for a new passport with which they can go through the relevant visa formalities at the entry and exit administrative department of the police station.

Holders of residence permits who replace their lost passport should apply for a change of passport number on their residence certificates.

- Losing luggage

1. Luggage lost during the flight to China

In this case, the airline company, which your airliner belongs to, shall usually bear the responsibility.

You can carry out lost and claim procedures in the lost property register office at the airport, showing your air ticket and luggage card. Give a detailed description as to the departure, transfer station, the amount of luggage, as well as the size, shape, color, mark and feature of the lost luggage, and fill in the lost property register form. Leave your convenient contact methods and take the telephone number and the contact name of the register office. For your convenient contact, you should also take down the address and telephone number of relevant offices affiliated to the airline company.

In case of confirmation of the lost, you can claim for compensation from the relevant airline company.

2. Luggage lost in China

If you are sure of the arrival of the luggage and its entry into the hotel, it's most likely that the porter mistook the floors, rooms or travel groups, and you can ask the guide or the hotel staff for help. If the luggage is lost on the way to hotel, you can call the police by dialing 110, and the policemen of China will try their best to help you find the luggage. Since detailed clues offered by the owner will better help search the lost property, you should ask for invoices when taking a taxi or shopping. Maybe they can provide valuable clues for the police.

Key Sentences

1. I lost my passport (traveler's check).

2. I don't know where I lost it.

3. I left it on the taxi.

4. I think someone stole it from me.

5. Here is the number of my traveler's check (passport).

6. I want to report the loss in a proper form.

7. I want to fill in a disembarkation confirmation letter.

8. Where is the British embassy (consulate)?

9. Please contact this address if it is found.

10. Please help me find what I've lost.

应用会话 yīng yòng huì huà

1. 我 丢 了 护 照（旅 行 支 票）。
Wǒ diū le hù zhào (lǚ xíng zhī piào).

2. 不 知 道 丢 在 哪 里 了。
Bù zhī dào diū zài nǎ lǐ le.

3. 落 在 出 租 汽 车 后 下 车 了。
Là zài chū zū qì chē hòu xià chē le.

4. 好 像 是 在 什 么 地 方 被 骗 走 了。
Hǎo xiàng shì zài shén me dì fāng bèi piàn zǒu le.

5. 这 是 旅 行 支 票（护 照）号 码。
Zhè shì lǚ xíng zhī piào (hù zhào) hào mǎ.

6. 我 想 填 写 遗 失（被 盗）证 明 书。
Wǒ xiǎng tián xiě yí shī (bèi dào) zhèng míng shū.

7. 我 想 填 写 入 境 确 认 书。
Wǒ xiǎng tián xiě rù jìng què rèn shū.

8. 英 国 大 使 馆（领 事 馆）在 哪 儿？
Yīng guó Dà shǐ guǎn (Lǐng shì guǎn) zài nǎr?

9. 如 果 找 到 的 话，请 和 这 个 地 址 联 系。
Rú guǒ zhǎo dào de huà, qǐng hé zhè gè dì zhǐ lián xì.

10. 请 帮 我 找 遗 失 品。
Qǐng bāng wǒ zhǎo yí shī pǐn.

Theft and Fire

Fire! Could someone please help?

着火了！有谁来帮忙

zháo huǒ le!yǒu shuí lái bāng máng

New Words

- fire 火灾 huǒ zāi
- thief 小偷 xiǎo tōu
- robber 强盗 qiáng dào
- cutpurse 扒手 pá shǒu
- public security bureau 公安局 gōng ān jú
- police officer 警官 jǐng guān
- police 警察 jǐng chá
- fire brigade 消防队 xiāo fáng duì
- fire extinguisher 灭火器 miè huǒ qì
- witness 目击者 mù jī zhě
- embassy 大使馆 dà shǐ guǎn
- consulate 领事馆 lǐng shì guǎn
- a theft report 被盗证明书 bèi dào zhèng míng shū

1. Shout for help when your life is in danger, "jiùmìng"(Help)!
2. Shout "qiǎngjié"(robbery) when somebody robs your purse or wallet.
3. It's better to keep your valuable properties at the safe deposit of your hotel.

Key Sentences

1. Help please!

2. Fire!/Stop thief!

3. Pickpocket!

4. Hello! Is that the service desk? Please ask for the police.

5. Where is the fire extinguisher (emergency exit)?

6. Please take me to the nearest police station.

7. My purse has been stolen.

8. My handbag was snatched.

9. Please contact the embassy.

10. I want to talk to someone who speaks English.

应用会话 yīng yòng huì huà

1. 请 帮 忙 ！

Qǐng bāng máng!

2. 火 灾 ！ / 小 偷 ！

Huǒ zāi! / Xiǎo tōu!

3. 扒 手 ！

Pá shǒu!

4. 喂 ，服 务 台 吗 ？ 请 叫 警 察 来 。

Wèi, fú wù tái ma? Qǐng jiào jǐng chá lái.

5. 灭 火 器 （ 紧 急 出 口 ）在 哪 儿 ？

Miè huǒ qì (jǐn jí chū kǒu) zài nǎr?

6. 请 把 我 带 到 离 这 儿 最 近 的 公 安 局 。

Qǐng bǎ wǒ dài dào lí zhèr zuì jìn de gōng ān jú.

7. 我 的 钱 包 被 偷 走 了 。

Wǒ de qián bāo bèi tōu zǒu le.

8. 我 的 手 提 包 被 抢 走 了 。

Wǒ de shǒu tí bāo bèi qiǎng zǒu le.

9. 请 联 系 大 使 馆 。

Qǐng lián xì dà shǐ guǎn.

10. 我 要 请 会 说 英 语 的 人 。

Wǒ yào qǐng huì shuō Yīng yǔ de rén.

Traffic Accidents

There has been a car accident.

发生了车祸

fā shēng le chē huò

New Words

· car	汽车 qì chē	· ambulance	救护车 jiù hù chē
· flat tire	放炮 fàng pào	· interpreter	翻译 fān yì
· malfunction	故障 gù zhàng	· contact	联系 lián xì
· car accident	车祸 chē huò	· responsibility	责任 zé rèn
· police	警察 jǐng chá	· fault	错误 cuò wù

Tips for Trips

1. The driver's seat in automobiles in China is on the left, and cars drive on the right side of the street.
2. Number of private vehicles in China is on the rise. Roads are almost always blocked during rush hours.
3. Travelers will not receive special punishment when the accident is relatively minor, but in case of a serious accident, you'd better get in touch with your embassy or consulate in China.
   Embassy of the United States of America
   Chancery: No.3, Xiushui North Road, Jiangoumen Wai
   TEL:65323431
   Embassy of the United Kingdom of Great Britain and Northern Ireland Chancery: No.11, Guanghua Road
   TEL:65321961
   Embassy of Canada
   Chancery: No19, Dongzhimen Road, Chaoyang District
   TEL: 65323536
   Embassy of Australia
   Chancery: No.21, Dongzhimen Wai Road, Sanlitun
   TEL: 65322331-7

Key Sentences

1. One of the car's tires is flat.

2. There is a problem with the car. It won't move.

3. There has been a car accident .

4. Please call an ambulance quickly.

5. I don't speak Chinese. Please call a policeman.

6. Please ask for an English interpreter.

7. Please contact the embassy (consulate).

8. Will you please contact this place (person)?

9. I'm not responsible for this.

10. It's not my fault.

应用会话 yīng yòng huì huà

1. 汽车的轮胎放炮了。

   Qì chē de lún tāi fàng pào le.

2. 汽车发生了故障，走不动了。

   Qì chē fā shēng le gù zhàng, zǒu bú dòng le.

3. 发生了车祸。

   Fā shēng le chē huò.

4. 请赶快叫救护车来。

   Qǐng gǎn kuài jiào jiù hù chē lái.

5. 我不会说中文，请叫警察来。

   Wǒ bú huì shuō Zhōng wén, qǐng jiào jǐng chá lái.

6. 请叫英文翻译来。

   Qǐng jiào Yīng wén fān yì lái.

7. 请和大使馆（领事馆）联系。

   Qǐng hé dà shǐ guǎn (lǐng shì guǎn) lián xì.

8. 请联系这个地方（人），好吗？

   Qǐng lián xì zhè gè dì fang (rén), hǎo ma?

9. 没有我的错。

   Méi yǒu wǒ de cuò.

10. 不是我的错误（过失）。

    Bú shì wǒ de cuò wù (guò shī).

At an Emergency

Please take me to the nearest hospital.

请到附近医院

qǐng dào fù jìn yī yuàn

New Words

- acute disease 急性病 jí xìng bìng
- disease 病 bìng
- hurt 受伤 shòu shāng
- physical situation 身体情况 shēn tǐ qíng kuàng
- abdomen 肚子 dù zi
- stomach 胃 wèi
- head 头 tóu
- tooth 牙 yá
- hospital 医院 yī yuàn
- doctor 医生 yī shēng
- medicine 药 yào
- ambulance 救护车 jiù hù chē

If you have indigestion or a critical health problem, contact the information desk of your hotel and ask for help immediately.

Key Sentences

1. Hello? Is that the service desk? Can someone please hurry here?
2. I have a horrible pain and can hardly move.
3. Please help me.
4. Please call the ambulance.
5. Please send for a doctor quickly.
6. I have a terrible stomach (tooth) ache.
7. Something wrong happened to me suddenly.
8. It's almost killing me.
9. Will you please contact my doctor?
10. Please escort me to the hospital.

应用会话 yīng yòng huì huà

1. 喂，是服务台吗？请快点儿来好吗？
   Wèi, shì fú wù tái ma? Qǐng kuài diǎnr lái hǎo ma?

2. 我疼得很厉害，一点儿也不能动。
   Wǒ téng de hěn lì hài, yì diǎnr yě bù néng dòng.

3. 请帮帮我。
   Qǐng bāng bāng wǒ.

4. 请叫救护车。
   Qǐng jiào jiù hù chē.

5. 请快叫医生来看看。
   Qǐng kuài jiào yī shēng lái kàn kàn.

6. 肚子（牙）疼得很厉害。
   Dù zi (yá) téng de hěn lì hài.

7. 身体突然不舒服了。
   Shēn tǐ tū rán bù shū fú le.

8. 快要我的命了。
   Kuài yào wǒ de mìng le.

9. 请跟我医生那儿联系好吗？
   Qǐng gēn wǒ yī shēng nàr lián xì hǎo ma?

10. 请你陪我去医院。
    Qǐng nǐ péi wǒ qù yī yuàn.

Seeing the Doctor

I want to see the doctor.

我要看病

wǒ yào kàn bìng

New Words

- diagnosis and treatment 诊疗 zhěn liáo
- first diagnose 初诊 chū zhěn
- emergency patient 急性病人 jí xìng bìng rén
- nurse 护士 hù shi
- operation 手术 shǒu shù
- mouth 嘴 zuǐ
- eye 眼睛 yǎn jīng
- throat 嗓子 sǎng zi
- nose 鼻子 bí zi
- ear 耳朵 ěr duo
- hand 手 shǒu
- foot 脚 jiǎo
- back 背 bèi
- shoulder 肩膀 jiān bǎng

Tips for Trips

1. Clinics for foreigners are set up specially in Chinese hospitals.
2. The diagnosis fees for foreigners are different from that of local residents.
   Following is the charge difference between Chinese people and foreigners:
   - A simple diagnosis fee for Chinese is ¥15
   - A simple diagnosis fee for foreigners is ¥16
3. The cost for a Chinese person is nearly ¥100 for medicines and injection relating to having a cold.

Key Sentences

1. I want to register.

2. I am a tourist from the US and this is my first visit to the country.

3. I have no reservations. I am an emergency patient.

4. I want to have an emergency treatment.

5. I want to see a doctor who speaks French (English).

6. I am hurt.

7. I broke my leg (shoulder).

8. I am in a very awful state.

9. I was in a traffic accident.

10. A thug suddenly attacked me.

应用会话 yīng yòng huì huà

1. 我要挂号。
   Wǒ yào guà hào.

2. 我是从美国来的游客，第一次来这里。
   Wǒ shì cóng Měi guó lái de yóu kè, dì yī cì lái zhè lǐ.

3. 我没有预约，是急诊病人。
   Wǒ méi yǒu yù yuē, shì jí zhěn bìng rén.

4. 我要看急诊。
   Wǒ yào kàn jí zhěn.

5. 我要会说法语（英语）的医生。
   Wǒ yào huì shuō Fǎ yǔ (Yīng yǔ) de yī shēng.

6. 我受伤了。
   Wǒ shòu shāng le.

7. 腿（肩膀）摔断了。
   Tuǐ (jiān bǎng) shuāi duàn le.

8. 我觉得身体非常不好。
   Wǒ jué de shēn tǐ fēi cháng bù hǎo.

9. 我遇到交通事故了。
   Wǒ yù dào jiāo tōng shì gù le.

10. 流氓突然袭击了我。
    Liú máng tū rán xí jī le wǒ.

Diagnosis

Is it serious?

不要紧吗

bú yào jǐn ma

New Words

- pneumonia 肺炎 fèi yán
- headache 头疼 tóu téng
- sneeze 打喷嚏 dǎ pēn ti
- stomachache 肚子疼 dù zi téng
- constipation 便秘 biàn mì
- bone fracture 骨折 gǔ zhé
- appendicitis 盲肠炎 máng cháng yán
- infectious disease 传染病 chuán rǎn bìng
- toothache 牙疼 yá téng
- blood pressure 血压 xuè yā
- pulse 脉博 mài bó
- temperature 体温 tǐ wēn
- fever 发烧 fā shāo
- hospitalize 住院 zhù yuàn
- leave the hospital 出院 chū yuàn
- sickroom 病房 bìng fáng

1. Foreigners will spend three times more than the locals on medical treatment.
2. To save on medical treatment fee, it's best to buy travel insurance at the airport before going abroad. Keep the invoice issued by the hospital, so that you can ask for compensation after going back.

Key Sentences

1. I drank a little bit too much yesterday.

2. It feels like food poisoning.

3. I caught a cold.

4. My limbs feel weak and aching.

5. I have a fever.

6. I have a headache, a terrible headache.

7. Loose bowels.

8. Very nauseous.

9. I have no appetite.

10. I have a sore throat.

应用会话 yīng yòng huì huà

1. 昨 天 我 喝 多 了 点 儿 。
   Zuó tiān wǒ hē duō le diǎnr.

2. 我 觉 得 是 食 物 中 毒 。
   Wǒ jué de shì shí wù zhòng dú.

3. 我 患 了 感 冒 。
   Wǒ huàn le gǎn mào.

4. 全 身 酸 软 ， 没 有 力 气 。
   Quán shēn suān ruǎn, méi yǒu lì qi.

5. 我 发 烧 。
   Wǒ fā shāo.

6. 头 疼 ，疼 得 要 命 。
   Tóu téng, téng de yào mìng.

7. 拉 肚 子 。
   Lā dù zi.

8. 很 恶 心 。
   Hěn ě xīn.

9. 没 有 胃 口 。
   Méi yǒu wèi kǒu.

10. 嗓 子 疼 。
    Sǎng zi téng.

Key Sentences

11. I have a stopped-up nose.

12. I cannot breathe properly.

13. The blood type is A (AB, O).

14. It's allergy.

15. I have rather high (low) blood pressures.

16. There are symptoms of diabetes.

17. Is it serious?

18. Can I continue to tour around?

19. How long roughly will I be hospitalized?

20. Please give me my diagnosis record.

11. 鼻 子 不 通 气 。
Bí zi bù tōng qì.

12. 喘 不 上 气 来 。
Chuǎn bú shàng qì lái.

13. 血 型 是 A （ AB ， O ） 型 。
Xuè xíng shì A (AB, O) xíng.

14. 有 过 敏 症 。
Yǒu guò mǐn zhèng.

15. 我 的 血 压 比 较 高 （ 低 ） 。
Wǒ de xuè yā bǐ jiào gāo (dī).

16. 有 糖 尿 病 症 状 。
Yǒu táng niào bìng zhèng zhuàng.

17. 不 要 紧 吗 ？
Bú yào jǐn ma?

18. 可 以 继 续 旅 游 吗 ？
Kě yǐ jì xù lǚ yóu ma?

19. 大 约 住 院 多 久 ？
Dà yuē zhù yuàn duō jiǔ?

20. 请 给 我 诊 断 书 。
Qǐng gěi wǒ zhěn duàn shū.

At the Drugstores

Please give me some medicine for my cold.

请给我感冒药

qǐng gěi wǒ gǎn mào yào

New Words

- drugstore 药店 yào diàn
- medicine for cold 感冒药 gǎn mào yào
- medicine for headache 头疼药 tóu téng yào
- medicine for stomach 胃肠药 wèi cháng yào
- injury relief 受伤药 shòu shāng yào
- Chinese medicine 中药 zhōng yào
- medicine for cough 咳嗽药 ké sòu yào
- medicine for diarrhea 止泻药 zhǐ xiè yào
- medicine for carsickness 晕车药 yùn chē yào
- aspirin 阿司匹林 ā sī pǐ lín
- vitamin 维他命 wéi tā mìng

Tips for Trips

1. The prices of some commonly-used medicine are as following:
   - Digestant △6.30 yuan for 100 pills
   - Rubberized fabric △2.50 yuan/per case
   - Headache medicine △2.50 yuan for 24 pills
   - Anti-diarrhea △2.00 yuan for 24 pills
   - Colds medicine △12.00 yuan for 10 pills
2. Prepare some common medicines before going abroad.

Key Sentences

1. Have you got any medicine for colds?

2. I am allergic to penicillin.

3. Please give me some medicine for my toothache.

4. Do you have anything good for eye diseases?

5. Please give me some vitamins.

6. Please give me some health drinks.

7. Please give me some medicine for my headache (cold/ diarrhea).

8. Please let me have some medicine for external use.

9. Please give me some medicine for wounds due to falls or strains.

10. How much are these all together?

应用会话 yīng yòng huì huà

1. 有 没 有 感 冒 药 ？
Yǒu méi yǒu gǎn mào yào?

2. 我 对 盘 尼 西 林 过 敏 。
Wǒ duì pán ní xī lín guò mǐn.

3. 请 给 我 牙 疼 药 。
Qǐng gěi wǒ yá téng yào.

4. 有 没 有 好 的 眼 药 ？
Yǒu méi yǒu hǎo de yǎn yào?

5. 请 给 我 维 他 命 。
Qǐng gěi wǒ wéi tā mìng.

6. 请 给 我 健 康 饮 料 。
Qǐng gěi wǒ jiàn kāng yǐn liào.

7. 请 给 我 头 疼 药（感 冒 药 、止 泻 药）。
Qǐng gěi wǒ tóu téng yào (gǎn mào yào, zhǐ xiè yào).

8. 请 给 我 外 敷 药 。
Qǐng gěi wǒ wài fū yào.

9. 请 给 我 跌 倒 或 是 扭 伤 时 用 的 药 ？
Qǐng gěi wǒ diē dǎo huò shì niǔ shāng shí yòng de yào?

10. 一 共 多 少 钱 ？
Yí gòng duō shǎo qián?

Reservation/Reconfirming Flight

I want to confirm my reservation.

我要确认预订

wǒ yào què rèn yù dìng

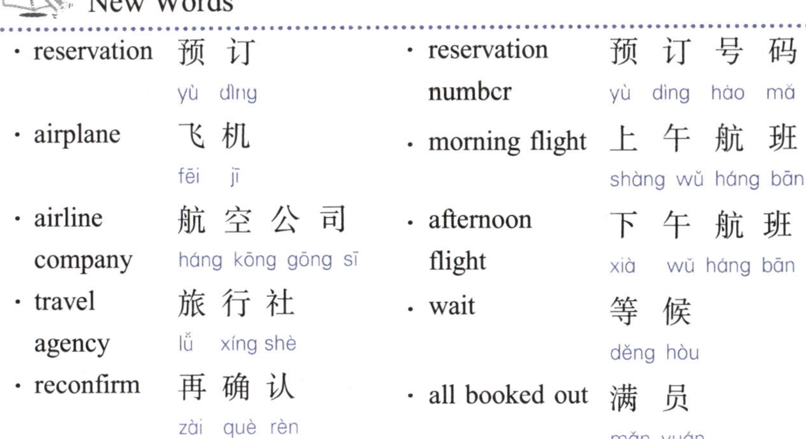

New Words

English	Chinese	Pinyin
reservation	预订	yù dìng
airplane	飞机	fēi jī
airline company	航空公司	háng kōng gōng sī
travel agency	旅行社	lǚ xíng shè
reconfirm	再确认	zài què rèn
reservation numbcr	预订号码	yù dìng hào mǎ
morning flight	上午航班	shàng wǔ háng bān
afternoon flight	下午航班	xià wǔ háng bān
wait	等候	děng hòu
all booked out	满员	mǎn yuán

Tips for Trips

1. A round ticket bought before going aboard has to be reconfirmed in 72 hours after reaching the travel destination. If not, the order can be canceled, so make sure you confirm the ticket.
2. It is troublesome for the ticket booker to board, so call the airline company at any time to emphasize you do want to be on board, the airline company may arrange the seat for you preferentially.

3. The following are some representative offices of English speaking countries' airline companies :

Beijing office of the US Northwest Airlines

Tel:	010-65051353
Address:	501A West Wing, CWTC, Beijing
Office hours:	Mon.~Fri.: 8:30 ~ 17:30
	Closed on Sat. and Sun.

Beijing office of the US United Airlines

Tel:	010-64631111
Address:	Ground floor,North Gate of Lufthunsa Friendship Shopping Mall
Office hours:	Mon.~Fri.: 9:00~18:00
	Sat. and Sun.: 9:00~13:00

Beijing office of Canadian Inte'l Airlines

Tel:	010-64682001
Address:	C201 Beijing Lufthunsa Center
Office hours:	Mon.~Fri.: 9:00~17:30
	Sat.: 9:00~13:00
	Closed on Sun.

Beijing office of British Airlines

Tel:	010-85115599
Address:	210 Scitech Tower, 22 Jianguomenwai Avenue, Beijing
Office hours:	Mon.~Fri.: 9:00~17:00
	Sat.: 9:00~12:00
	Closed on Sun.

Beijing office of German Lufthansa Airlines

Tel:	010-64654488
Address:	S101 Lufthunsa Center
Office hours:	Mon.~Fri.: 9:00~17:30
	Sat.: 9:00~12:00
	Closed on Sun.

Beijing office of French Airlines

Tel:	010-85115599
Address:	512 Full Link Tower, Beijing
Office hours:	Mon.~Fri.: 9:00~17:15
	Sat. and Sun.: 9:00~12:00

Beijing office of AZ Italian Airlines

Tel:	010-65672299
Address:	1828 China Merchants Tower, 118 Jianguo Road
Office hours:	Mon.~Fri.: 9:00~17:30
	Closed on Sat. and Sun.

 **Key Sentences**

1. Hello. I would like to book an air ticket.

2. Are there vacancies on the flight from Beijing to New York in the morning of May 10th?

3. I want to reserve my seat on the flight from Beijing to New York.

4. Please reserve a seat for me on the flight in the morning of May 10th.

5. Please add my name to the list of passengers for seat reservation.

6. My name is Mike Smith.

7. What's the reservation number?

8. What is the flight number, and when does it take off?

9. When does it arrive in New York?

10. I would like to reconfirm my reservation for flight 702 on US Northwest on May 10th.

应用会话 yīng yòng huì huà

1. 喂，我要预订班机。
Wèi, wǒ yào yù dìng bān jī.

2. 5月10日上午自北京飞往纽约的航班，有座位吗？
Wǔ yuè shí rì shàng wǔ zì Běi jīng fēi wǎng Niǔ yuē de háng bān, yǒu zuò wèi ma?

3. 我要预订自北京飞往纽约的班机。
Wǒ yào yù dìng zì Běi jīng fēi wǎng Niǔ yuē de bān jī.

4. 拜托，订5月10日上午的班机。
Bài tuō, dìng Wǔ yuè shí rì shàng wǔ de bān jī.

5. 请把我登到预订机票者的名单上。
Qǐng bǎ wǒ dēng dào yù dìng jī piào zhě de míng dān shàng.

6. 我名字叫迈克·史密斯，英语是Mike~。
Wǒ míng zì jiào Mài kè Shǐ mì sī, Yīng yǔ shì Mike~.

7. 预订号码是几号？
Yù dìng hào mǎ shì jǐ hào?

8. 几点起飞的几号航班？
Jǐ diǎn qǐ fēi de jǐ hào háng bān?

9. 几点到纽约？
Jǐ diǎn dào Niǔ yuē?

10. 我要再查对一下，5月10日美西北702次航班。
Wǒ yào zài chá duì yí xià, Wǔ yuè shí rì Měi xī běi qī líng èr cì háng bān.

Changing/Canceling Flight Reservations

I want to cancel my reservation.

我想退订

wǒ xiǎng tuì dìng

New Words

· change	更 改 gèng gǎi	· time	时 间 shí jiān
· cancel a reservation	退 订 tuì dìng	· what time	几 点 jǐ diǎn
· flight	航 班 háng bān	· other flights	别 的 航 班 bié de háng bān
· fly to New York	飞 往 纽 约 fēi wǎng Niǔ yuē	· the next flight	下 次 航 班 xià cì háng bān
· date	日 期 rì qī		

Tips for Trips

1. Put forward your request to the relevant person in time if you want to alter the date and the time of your return flight.
2. If you discover that the airline company is already closed for the day, please hold on and leave a message with your contact telephone number and room number. The airline company will contact you the next morning.

Key Sentences

1. I want to change my ticket scheduled for flight 702 on August 8th.

2. Can I change it for a flight on August 7th?

3. Can I change it for a morning (afternoon) flight?

4. I want to switch my morning flight for an afternoon one.

5. I want to switch my New York flight to Los Angeles.

6. I want to change my departure site from Beijing to Tianjin.

7. I want to change it for the same day.

8. A flight on a different airline will also do.

9. I want to cancel my reservation for flight 702 on August 8th.

10. My reservation number is 1234.

应用会话 yīng yòng huì huà

1. 我要换一下8月8日702次航班机票。

   Wǒ yào huàn yí xià Bā yuè bā rì qī líng èr cì háng bān jī piào.

2. 可以换成8月7日的吗？

   Kě yǐ huàn chéng Bā yuè qī rì de ma?

3. 可以换成上午（下午）的吗？

   Kě yǐ huàn chéng shàng wǔ (xià wǔ) de ma?

4. 我要把上午的换成下午的航班。

   Wǒ yào bǎ shàng wǔ de huàn chéng xià wǔ de háng bān.

5. 我要把飞往纽约的换成洛杉矶的。

   Wǒ yào bǎ fēi wǎng Niǔ yuē de huàn chéng Luò shān jī de.

6. 我要把北京登机换成天津。

   Wǒ yào bǎ Běi jīng dēng jī huàn chéng Tiān jīn.

7. 我要换同一天的。

   Wǒ yào huàn tóng yì tiān de.

8. 别的航空公司也可以。

   Bié de háng kōng gōng sī yě kě yǐ.

9. 我要退8月8日702次航班的预订票。

   Wǒ yào tuì Bā yuè bā rì qī líng èr cì háng bān de yù dìng piào.

10. 预订号码是1234。

    Yù dìng hào mǎ shì yī èr sān sì.

Departure from China

Please let me have a seat by the window.

请给我靠窗口的座位

qǐng gěi wǒ kào chuāng kǒu de zuò wèi

New Words

- counter 柜台 guì tái
- passport 护照 hù zhào
- air ticket 机票 jī piào
- luggage 行李 xíng li
- handle with care 注意搬运 zhù yì bān yùn
- on schedule 正点 zhèng diǎn
- take off 起飞 qǐ fēi
- board the plane 登机 deng ji
- boarding pass 登机牌 dēng jī pái
- go abroad 出国 chū guó
- procedures 手续 shǒu xù
- boarding gate 登机口 dēng jī kǒu
- tax-free shop 免税店 miǎn shuì diàn
- shopping 购物 gòu wù

Tips for Trips

1. If your luggage is not packed properly, the staff workers of the airport will repack it and charge 10 yuan.
2. Passengers taking Hong Kong, Macao or international flight must pay RMB¥90 each for the airport fee, children who are 12 years old or younger do not pay the airport fees; international passengers who transfer to flights at domestic airports, and stay within the quarantine zone, are exempted from the airport fees.

   In case you lose any articles at the Beijing Capital International Airport, please contact the Inquire Office for Lost Articles. Address: Room 12026, Gate 15, ground floor of the Navigation Station Building. Contact: Police Station of Beijing Capital International Airport.

   Inquiry tel.: 64564119, 64598333;

   In case your belongings are lost on any flight, please contact airline office directly.

   Flight information inquiry tel.: 2580

   Complaint-registration tel. of the Beijing Capital International Airport Co, Ltd: 64571666.

Key Sentences

1. Where is the US Northwest airline counter?

2. The luggage shall be consigned by air.

3. Please paste a "handle with care" label on it.

4. Could you please give me a seat by the gate?

5. Please help me find my luggage quickly.

6. Has Northwest Airline flight 702 taken off?

7. Roughly what time will it arrive?

8. What time shall boarding begin?

9. Where are procedures for going abroad handled?

10. Could you tell me where the tax-free shop is?

应用会话 yīng yòng huì huà

1. 美 西 北 航 空 公 司 柜 台 在 哪 儿 ？

   Měi Xī běi háng kōng gōng sī guì tái zài nǎr?

2. 这 都 是 托 运 的 行 李 。

   Zhè dōu shì tuō yùn de xíng li.

3. 请 贴 上"注 意 搬 运"标 签 。

   Qǐng tiē shàng"zhù yì bān yùn"biāo qiān.

4. 请 给 我 门 口 旁 边 的 座 位 好 吗 ？

   Qǐng gěi wǒ mén kǒu páng biān de zuò wèi hǎo ma?

5. 能 帮 我 快 一 点 儿 取 到 行 李 吗 。

   Néng bāng wǒ kuài yì diǎnr qǔ dào xíng li ma.

6. 美 西 北 702 次 航 班 已 经 起 飞 了 吗 ？

   Měi Xī běi qī líng èr cì háng bān yǐ jīng qǐ fēi le ma?

7. 大 约 在 几 点 到 达 ？

   Dà yuē zài jǐ diǎn dào dá?

8. 几 点 开 始 登 机 ？

   Jǐ diǎn kāi shǐ dēng jī?

9. 在 哪 儿 办 出 国 手 续 ？

   Zài nǎr bàn chū guó shǒu xù?

10. 请 问 ，免 税 店 在 哪 儿 ？

    Qǐng wèn, miǎn shuì diàn zài nǎr?

第3章

Travel Information

A General Survey of China

◆ Location

China lies in the eastern part of Asia, to the west coast of the Pacific Ocean, and borders North Korea, Russia, Kazakhstan, Kirghizstan, Tajikistan, Mongolia, Afghanistan, Pakistan, India, Laos, Nepal, Sikkim, Bhutan, Burma, and Vietnam. China is also on the opposite sea coast of Japan, South Korea, Philippines, Malaysia, Brunei, and Indonesia.

◆ Geography

China has an area of 9.6 million square kilometers, which is the largest national territory in Asia.

The geographical shape of China is like a ladder, which drops southward step by step from the east to the west. The percentage of different kinds of terrain is as follow: mountains 33%, plateaus 26%, hills 10%, basins 19%, and plain 12%.

◆ Weather

The weather in China is very complicated; most parts of China lie in the North Temperate Zone and the subtropical zone, which belong to the continental monsoon climate. The majority of China has four clearly demarcated seasons, hot in summer and cold in winter.

Because of the vast territory, varied topography and the discrepancy in elevation, there are various weather types. The climate zones in China, from the south to the north, are the tropical zone, the subtropical zone, the warm zone, the medium warm zone, the cold warm zone, and additionally, the perpendicular temperate zone in the Tibetan Plateau.

The Mohe River area in Heilongjiang Province is the northern-most part of China, which lies to the north of the latitude 53°N , and belongs to the cold warm climate. The Zengmu'ansha Reef in Hainan Province is the southernmost part of China, 400 kilometers away from the equator and having an equatorial climate. There is great temperature variance between the north and the south. In winter, most parts of China are covered with ice and heavy snow. The average temperature of the Mohe River in January is about -30℃, but at the same time the average temperatures of Sanya in Hainan exceeds 20℃. In winter most areas are very cold and there is a great difference in temperature from the north to the south. In summer, when the sun shines directly on the northern hemisphere, the North experiences a longer daytime and will receive more or less the same heat and sunshine as compared to the South. Therefore, except for the extremely high Qinghai-Tibet Plateau, most areas of the country have a high temperature, and the temperature difference between the north and the south is not so obvious.

Rainfall is not distributed evenly in terms of terrain and time in most parts of China. Rain falls more in the east and less in the west,

reducing gradually from the southeast to the northwest, and falls more in summers. The rainy season in the south is long, and focused on May to October. The rainy season in the north is shorter, focused in June and July. Some years have much rain while some years have little rain, and variance among years is great.

◆ Administrative Distribution

The administrative distribution of China consists of provinces, cities (counties) and villages (towns). Upper levels are in charge of lower ones. There are 34 provincial units, which consist of 23 provinces, four municipalities directly under the Central Government, five autonomous regions, and two special administrative zones.

◆ Population

China has the largest population in the world, 1,276 million(2001), which makes up 20% of that of the whole world. There are 56 ethnic groups all in all, and the Han accounts for 92%. Mandarin is commonly used. The government permits free religion; generally people believe in Buddhism, Taoism, Islam, and Christianity, etc.

Information for Tourists in China

◆ China Post

You can mail postcards, ordinary mail or global special deliveries to anywhere in the world and at any time in any hotel, but printing and parcels must be posted in the appointed post office. Many shops can also consign their commodities for their customers.

If you want to send a fax or make a telephone call, you may go to the commercial center in hotels.

Expenses of international fax:

(1) Charges for international fax are calculated according to the actual number of pages that the customer dispatches (receiving a fax is free), and not according to the characters on each page.

(2) Basic expenses

The expenses of page one are: mail-handling fees plus the usage fees of international long-distance for three minutes, among them: the mail-handling fees are ¥37. The pages following cost: handling fees plus the usage fees of international long-distance for one minute, among them: the mail-handling fee is ¥22.

◆ Telephone Calls

In most cases, you are able to make domestic or international calls from your own hotel room, and accounts are settled when checking out. When you are in a downtown area visiting scenic spots, shops or recreational places, you can make international calls or domestic calls at nearby post offices or public telephone booths. Expenses are paid after the call is concluded. When dialing domestic long-distance calls, first dial regional numbers, then dial the number wanted. Regional numbers of the main cities are: Beijing (010), Shanghai (021), Tianjin (022), Guangzhou (020), Guilin (0773), Hangzhou (0571), Kunming (0871), Xi'an (029). When dialing international long-distance calls, first dial the international dialing code "00" and the national serial number, then dial area code (remove "0" if the first number of the area codes is "0"), lastly, dial the number wanted.

◆ Electricity Supply

Most of the electricity power inside China is alternating current about 220V. Many medium and top star hotels are equipped with transformation connector sockets that can be used by electric shavers

and hair dryers.

◆ Water

Not all tap water can be drunk directly in China, but in cities bottled mineral water is available almost everywhere.

◆ Washing Room

In the streets or tourist spots in large and medium tourist cities, charge toilets are common and the charge is generally ¥0.2~0.3 each time. But washing rooms in airports, large-scaled shopping plazas are free. All public lavatories in Beijing are free.

◆ Currency of China

The currency of China is the RMB. The unit of RMB is the yuan (¥), and fractional currency is *jiao* and *fen*. One yuan equals ten *jiao*, and one *jiao* equals ten *fen*. *Jiao* and *fen* have paper forms, and there are also one-yuan, one-*jiao* and five-*jiao* coins. Yuan bills come in denominations of 1, 2, 5, 10, 20, 50, and 100 yuan. *Jiao* bills come in denominations of 1, 2, and 5 *jiao*, and the *fen* has 1, 2 , and 5 notes. The symbol of RMB is ¥.

◆ Foreign Currency

Currencies which are exchangeable or cashable in China:

U.S.dollar, Pound sterling, European Euro, Japanese yen, Australian dollar, Canadian dollar, Hong Kong dollar, Swiss Franc, Danmark kroner, Norway krone, Sweden krona, Singapore dollar, Malaysian dollar, Macao coin, etc. Banks handle the cash-in and cash-out business of foreign currencies.

According to China's current regulations of exchange control, foreign currency is forbidden to circulate and accounts cannot be closed in terms of foreign currencies in the territory of China. For the convenience of foreigners, the Bank of China and other authorized banks can not only exchange traveler's check in foreign currency and foreign credit cards into RMB, but also deal with the exchange of 22 kinds of foreign currencies and the Taiwanese New Taiwan dollar.

In addition, some hotels, restaurants or shops can exchange foreign currency into RMB in order to offer convenience to people who want to cash. Chinese currency which is not spent can be exchanged into foreign currency before travelers leave the territory with the Exchange Sheet effective within six months.

Different exchange rates are used in different situations when exchanging. The buying price is used when exchanging traveler's checks, credit cards, or remitting money; and the selling prices of foreign currencies are used when cashing out foreign currencies and foreign cash. Buying prices of foreign currencies are used when cashing in foreign cash.

Foreign credit cards which can be used in China:

At present, the foreign credit cards which are available in China are as follows:

1. Master Card
2. Visa Card
3. American Express Card
4. JCB card
5. Diners Card

◆ Useful Telephone Numbers

International directory inquiry	115
Long-distance directory inquiry	113, 173
Local directory inquiry	114
Fire alarm	119
City patrol police	110
First aid telephone	120

Beijing

Weather forecast: 12121

Taxi complaints: 68351150

Civil aviation information: 2580

Railway information: 2585

Railway ticket booking: 63217188

Airplane ticket booking: 2581

First-aid centers in Beijing: 120, 999

Int'l Medical Center, Beijing
Telephone : (010) 64651561, 64651562
Fax: (010) 64651984

Beijing Center of Asia Emergency Assistance
Telephone : (010)64629100, 64629112
Fax: (010) 64629111

International SOS Company, Beijing report center
Telephone : (010) 65003419, 65003388
Fax: (010) 65016048

Travel Rescue Center of China International Travel Service
Telephone: (010) 66031185
Fax: (010) 66012040
European first aid: 65053191 - 95

Shanghai

Weather: 12121

Shanghai ticket office of China East Airline Company: 62475953 (domestic), 62472255 (international)

Shanghai Airlines ticket office: 62681551

Rainbow Bridge International Airport, Shanghai: 62688918

Information counter of Railways, Shanghai: 63179090

Information counter of the passenger station: 63261261

Guangzhou

Weather: 12121

The medical command center of the first aid center, Guangzhou: 120

Information counter of the Cloud Airport: 86666123

International passenger transportation: 86661803

China South Airline Company's ticket office: 83312332

Information counter of the railway station, Guangzhou: 86661789

Taxi company, Guangzhou: 86662014

"Zhou Tou Zui" station, Guangzhou port (the line of Hong Kong and Macao): 8444949

The quality complaint telephone of travel

If you receive inequitable treatment while traveling within the boundaries of China's mainland, you can dial the following relevant telephones:

Quality Standard Management Department of National Tourism Administration

Fax: (010)65122096

Telephone: (010) 65234521

International Urgent Rescue Center of Public Health Ministry

Fax: (010)64001746

Telephone: (010) 64001746

National Supervisory Office of Tourism Quality

Hours of operation: 8:30~12:00 14:30~17:00

Phone number for complaints: (010) 65275315

Fax: (010) 65122096

Address: A 9 Jianguomennei Street, Beijing

Postcode: 100740

Supervisory Office of Tourism Quality in Beijing

Hours of operation: 8: 30~12:00 14:30~17:00

Phone number for complaints: (010) 65130828

Fax: (010) 65158251 65158255

Address: Room 1001 Travel Mansion,28 Jianguomenwai Street, Beijing

Postcode: 100022

Supervisory Office of Tourism Quality in Tianjin

Hours of operation: 8:30~17:30 18:30~8:30

Phone number for complaints: (022)28359093,28358812

Fax: (022) 28352324

Address: No. 18 Friendship Way, Hexi District, Tianjin

Postcode: 300074

Supervisory Office of Tourism Quality in Hebei Province

Hours of operation: 9:00~11:30 14:30~17:30

Phone number for complaints: (0311) 6014239 5814239

Fax: (0311) 6015368

Address: No. 22 Yucai Street, Shijiazhuang, Hebei Province

Postcode: 050021

Supervisory Office of Tourism Quality in Shanxi Province

Hours of operation: 8:30~11: 30 13:30~17:00

Phone number for complaints: (0351) 4047544, 4031616

Fax: (0351) 4048289

Address: No. 282 Yingze Street, Taiyuan, Shanxi Province

Postcode: 030001

Supervisory Office of Tourism Quality in Inner Mongolia Autonomous Region

Hours of operation: 8:00~12:00 14:00~18:00

Phone number for complaints: (0471) 6282653

Fax: (0471) 668561

Address: No. 1 Xinhua Street, Huhhot, the Inner Mongolia Autonomous Region

Postcode: 010055

Supervisory Office of Tourism Quality in Liaoning Province

Hours of operation: 24 hours

Phone number for complaints: (024) 86112228

Fax:(024)6809415

Address: No. 113 Yellow River Southern Street, Huanggu District, Shenyang, Liaoning Province

Postcode: 110031

Supervisory Office of Tourism Quality in Jilin Province

Hours of operation: 8:30~11:30 13:30~17:00

Phone number for complaints: (0431) 5653030

Fax: (0431) 5642053

Address: No. 14 Xinmin St., Changchun, Jilin Province
Postcode: 130021

Supervisory Office of Tourism Quality in Heilongjiang Province

Hours of operation: 8:00~17:00
Phone number for complaints: (0451) 2324162
Address: No. 4 Xidazhi Street, Nangang District, Harbin, Heilongjiang Province
Postcode: 150001

Supervisory Office of Tourism Quality in Shanghai

Hours of operation: 9:00~17:00
Phone number for complaints: (021)64390630, 64393615
Fax: (021) 64391159
Address: No. 2525 Zhongshanxi St., Shanghai
Postcode: 200030

Supervisory Office of Tourism Quality in Jiangsu

Hours of operation: 8:00~12:00 14:00~18:00
Phone number for complaints: (025)3301221, 3418185
Fax: (025)3328795
Address: 255 Zhongshan North Road, Nanjing, Jiangsu Province
Postcode: 210003

Supervisory Office of Tourism Quality in Zhejiang

Hours of operation: 8:30~11:30 14:00~17:00
Phone number for complaints: (0571) 5117419
Fax: (0571) 5156429
Address: No.1 Shihan Road, Hangzhou, Zhejiang Province

Postcode: 310007

Supervisory Office of Tourism Quality in Anhui

Hours of operation: 8:30~11:30 14:00~17:00

Phone number for complaints: (0551) 2821763

Fax: (0551) 2824001

Address: No.4 Meishan Road, Hefei, Anhui Province

Postcode: 230061

Supervisory office of Tourism Quality in Jiangxi

Hours of operation: 8:30~11:30 14:00~17:00

Phone number for complaints: (0791) 6269965

Fax: (0791) 6227860

Address: No.35 Fuzhou Road, Nanchang, Jiangxi Province

Postcode: 330006

Supervisory Office of Tourism Quality in Fujian

Hours of operation: 8:30~11:30 14:00~17:00

Phone number for complaints: (0591) 7535640

Fax: (0591) 7538758

Address: No.1 Daying Street of the Dongda Road, Fuzhou, Fujian Province

Postcode: 350001

Supervisory Office of Tourism Quality in Shandong

Hours of operation: 24 hours

Phone number for complaints: (0531) 2963423

Fax: (0531) 2964284

Address: No.88 Jingshi Road , Jinan, Shandong Province

Postcode: 250014

Supervisory Office of Tourism Quality in Henan

Hours of operation: 24 hours

Phone number for complaints: (0371) 5905110

Fax: (0371) 5955656

Address: No.16 Jinshui Road, Zhengzhou, Henan Province

Postcode: 450003

Supervisory Office of Tourism Quality in Hubei

Hours of operation: 8:00~18:00

Phone number for complaints: (027) 84818760

Fax: (027) 84822513

Address: No.2 Building of Hanyang Qinshiqiao Community, Wuhan, Hubei Province

Postcode: 430050

Supervisory Office of Tourism Quality in Hunan

Hours of operation: 24 hours

Phone number for complaints: (0731) 4717614

Fax: (0731) 4720348

Address: Tuanjie Road, Wulipai, Changsha, Hunan Province

Postcode: 410001

Supervisory Office of Tourism Quality in Guangdong

Hours of operation: 8:30~17:00

Phone number for complaints: (020) 86681163

Fax: (020) 86665039

Address: No 185, Huanshixi Road, Guangzhou, Guangdong Province

Postcode: 510010

Supervisory Office of Tourism Quality in Guangxi Autonomous Region

Hours of operation: 8:30~11:30 14:00~17:00

Phone number for complaints: (0771) 2612216

Fax: (0771) 2801041

Address: No 40 Xinmin Road, Nanning, Guangxi Autonomous Region

Postcode: 530012

Supervisory Office of Tourism Quality in Hainan

Hours of operation: 8:30~11:30 14:00~17:00

Phone number for complaints: (0898)5358451,8008768188

Fax: (0898) 5353074

Address: Room 606,Travel Agency Mansion, No.6 Haifu Road, Haikou, Hainan Province

Postcode: 570203

Supervisory Office of Tourism Quality in Chongqing

Hours of operation: 8:30~11:30 14:00~17:00

Phone number for complaints: (023) 63890134

Fax: (023) 3851448

Address: No.63 Dongzilanyazheng Street, Yuzhong district, Chongqing

Postcode: 400000

Supervisory Office of Tourism Quality in Sichuan

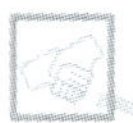

Hours of operation: 8:30~11:30 14:00~17:00

Phone number for complaints: (028) 6654780

Fax: (028) 6671042

Address: No.65, the second part of Renminnan road, Chengdu, Sichuan Province

Postcode: 530012

Supervisory Office of Tourism Quality in Guizhou

Hours of operation: 8:30~11:30 14:00~17:00

Phone number for complaints: (0851) 6818436

Fax: (0851) 6892309

Address: No.346-5, Zhonghuabei road, Guiyang, Guizhou Province (in the courtyard of the provincial government)

Postcode: 550001

Supervisory Office of Tourism Quality in Yunnan

Hours of operation: 8:00~17:00

Phone number for complaints: (0871) 3537361

Fax: (0871) 3174343

Address: No.218, Huanchengnan road, Kunming, Yunnan Province

Postcode: 650011

Supervisory Office of Tourism Quality in Tibet Autonomous Region

Hours of operation: Monday, Thursday and Friday mornings

Phone number for complaints: (0891) 6834193

Fax: (0891) 6334632

Address: No.208, Yuanlin Road, Lhasa, Tibet Autonomous Region

Postcode: 850001

Supervisory Office of Tourism Quality in Shaanxi

Hours of operation: 8:00~18:00

Phone number for complaints: (029)5261437

Fax: (029) 5250151, 5261437

Address: 15 Chang'an North Street, Xi'an, Shaanxi Province

Zipcode: 710061

Supervisory Office of Tourism Quality in Gansu

Hours of operation: 8:30~11:30 14:00~17:00

Phone number for complaints: (0931) 8826860

Fax: (0931) 8418443

Address: No.361, Tianshui Road, Lanzhou, Gunsu Province

Postcode: 730000

Supervisory Office of Tourism Quality in Qinghai

Hours of operation: 8:30~11:30 14:00~17:00

Phone number for complaints: (0971) 6159841

Fax: (0971) 8239515

Address: No.57, Xida Street, Xining, Qinghai Province

Postcode: 810000

Supervisory Office of Tourism Quality in Ningxia Autonomous Region

Hours of operation: 8:30~11:30 14:00~17:00

Phone number for complaints: (0951)5035449, 5064975

Fax: (0951) 6041783

Address: No.117, Jiefangxi Street, Yinchuan, Ningxia Autonomous Region

Postcode: 750001

Supervisory Office of Tourism Quality in Xinjiang Autonomous Region

Hours of operation: 9:30~13:30 16:00~20:00

Phone number for complaints: (0991) 2831902

Fax: (0991) 2824449

Address: No.6, Hetan Nan Road, Urumqi, Xinjiang Automous Region

Postcode: 830002

◆ Price Information for Travelers

The following price standards can help you understand China's local price situation.

Taxi	Initial price	10 yuan
Subway	1 person/per time	3 yuan
Bus	In-city line	1～2 yuan
Airport tax	International line	90 yuan
Airport tax	National line	50 yuan
Public telephone	3 minute	0. 3 yuan
Mabaral	1 pack	10 yuan
Newspaper	1 copy	1 yuan
Common magazine	1 copy	5 yuan
Noodles	1 bowl	5～10 yuan
Instant noodles	1 serving	3. 5～5 yuan
Bread	1 loaf	2～8 yuan
Hamburger (McDonald)	1	10 yuan
Coffee	1 glass(Starbucks)	10～30 yuan

Milk	1 package	3 yuan
Coca Cola	1 can	2 yuan
Beer	1 bottle	2 yuan
Beer	1 can	3～6 yuan
Ice creams (Helixes)	1	1～6 yuan
Gum	1 pack of 5 pieces	1.5 yuan
Film	1 roll(36 exposures)	18～25 yuan
Film developing	1 roll(36 exposures)	22～26 yuan
Dry cell battery	AA size	2～3 yuan
Petrol	1 liter	3～3.5 yuan

◆ World Heritage in China

Cultural heritage sites in China:

The Great Wall (Beijing)

The Palace Museum (Beijing)

Mogao Grottoes of Dunhuang (Gansu)

Mausoleum of Qin Shihuang and Museum of Terra Cotta Warriors (Shaanxi)

The Cave of Peking Man of Zhoukoudian (Beijing)

Chengde Mountain Resort and Temples (Hebei)

Mansion, Temple and Cemetery of Confucius in Qufu (Shandong)

Ancient Architectural Complex on Wudang Mountain (Hubei Province)

Potala Temple of Tibet (Tibet)

The Ancient City of Lijiang (Yunnan)

The Ancient City of Pingyao (Shanxi)

Ancient Gardens in Suzhou (Jiangsu)

The Summer Palace (Beijing)

The Temple of Heaven (Beijing)
The Imperial Mausoleum of the Ming and Qing Dynasties (Beijing)
The Longmen Grottoes (Henan)
Dazu Stone Carvings (Chongqing)
The Dujiang Weir -Qingcheng Mountain (Sichuan)
The Ancient Villages of South of Anhui——Xidi, Hongcun Villiage (Anhui)
Lushan Mountain Scenic Area (Jiangxi)

World Natural Heritage Sites in China

The Wulingyuan Scenic Area (Hunan)
The Jiuzaigou Ravine Scenic Area (Sichuan)
The Huanglong Scenic Area (Sichuan)

World Natural and Cultural Heritage in China

Taishan Mountain Scenic Area(Shandong)
Huangshan Mountain Scenic Area (Anhui)
Wuyi Mountain (Fujian)
Emei Mountain and Giant Buddha of Leshan(Sichuan)

◆ China's Main Festivals and Celebrations

New Year's Day——January 1st, Gregorian calendar
Spring Festival——Chinese lunar New Year (usually at the end of January or during February)
Lantern Festival——the 15th day of the first lunar month (15 days after the Spring Festival)
Qingming Festival——April 5th
May Day——May 1st
Children's Day——June 1st

Youth Day——May 4th

Dragon Boat Festival——the fifth day of the fifth lunar month

Commemoration Day of the Chinese Communist Party——July 1st

Commemoration Day of the return of Hong Kong——July 1st

Army Day——August 1st

Mid-autumn Festival——the 15th day of the eighth lunar month

National Day——October 1st

Chongyang Festival (Elderly Day)——the ninth day of the ninth lunar month

◆ Main Travel Festivals in China

Horseracing Festival, Qiangtang of Tibet

The Horseracing Festival is held in the Naqu area of Tibet Autonomous Region during the last ten days of August. Activities: Horseracing, archery match, horsemanship performance, singing and dancing performance, and exchange of goods.

Flambeau Festival of the Yi Minority, Yunnan.

The Flambeau Festival of the Yi Minority is held on June 24~26 in Shicun of the Lunan Yi Minority autonomous county, and Chuxiong City of the Yi Minority Autonomous State of Yunnan Province. Activities: *Yueqin* and *shengxiao* performances, the great *sanxuan* dance. There are other activities such as archery, horseracing, swing playing, corrida, wrestling, bonfire parties, etc.

Xuedun Festival, Tibet

The Xuedun Festival is held in Lhasa of the Tibet Autonomous Region in August (from the end of June to the beginning of August of the Zang Calendar). Activities: Xuedun (yoghurt) banquet, bathing

the Buddha in the sun, performance of the traditional Zang opera, trade fairs, and a visit to the South of Tibet.

The International Dragon Boat Festival, Yueyang

The International Dragon Boat Festival is held on the South Lake in Yueyang of Hunan Province from June 10th to 14th. The fifth day of the fifth lunar month is a traditional festival of China—the Dragon Boat Festival. Many places have the customs of dragon-boat races, eating *zongzi*, drinking yellow millet wine and hanging *ai* leaves, in order to mourn the great patriotic poet—Qu Yuan in ancient time. During these days, more than 20 dragon boat teams which come from the U.S.A., Canada, Australia and Southeast Asia will take part in the competition, and there are shows of dragon boat and folk customs, too.

Weifang International Kite Festival

The International Kite Festival is held in Weifang of Shandong Province from April 20th to the 25th. Weifang is recognized as "the kite city of the world". The headquarters of the International Kite Federation are located in the kite museum of Weifang. During the festival, there are opening ceremonies, kite flying ceremonies, an international kite match, a domestic kite match, the competition of the top-ten kites, and visiting kite museum.

The Peony Fair of Luoyang

The peony fair is held in Luoyang of Henan Province from April 15th to 25th. Luoyang peony planting has more than 1,400 years of history and there are more than 350 species. During the fair, the peonies will open competitively with rosy colors and fill the city with fragrance. There will be great art shows, too. Activities such as flower appreciation, lamp exhibitions, calligraphy and painting shows, photographic exhibitions, seminars, and consulting meetings will be held. People will also visit the Longmen Grottoes, White Horse Temple, Guan Lin, and ancient tomb museum.

The International Folk Song Festival in Guangxi

The International Folk Song Festival is held in Nanning or Liuzhou, Guangxi Autonomous Region on late April (the third day of the third lunar month) .

Activities: Chinese folk song competitions, Chinese and foreign folk song performances, etiquette performance and get-together parties for different nationalities. There will be a trade fair and touring too.

International Tourist Month of Wutai Mountain

International Tourist Month begins in the Taihuan town of the Wutai Mountain county, Shanxi Province from July 25th to August 25th.Wutai Mountain is one of the four Buddhist mountains of China.Big events will be held in the sixth lunar month annually. During these days, there will be activities like Buddhist ceremonies, folk recreational activities, and livestock trade fairs.

The International Volplane Festival of Jiayuguan

The International Volplane Festival will be held at the volplane base in Jiayuguan, Gansu Province from July 15th to 18th. Activities: Volplane matches, flight training—in order to get silver, golden or diamond badge. Pilots will take passengers into their planes, roaming the blue sky, enjoying the mystery of the Gobi desert, the ocean and the magnificent scenery of the snow-covered Qilian Mountain, as well as visiting Jiayuguan—the west end of the Great

Wall, Jiuquan and Dunhuang Mogao Grottoes.

The International Movie Festival in Changchun

The International Movie Festival is held in Changchun, Jilin Province from August 23rd to 28th. Activities: Grand film cultural activities, domestic and international movie star shows. Films from different countries and films which have won the "Changchun Commemorative Cup" will be shown and commented on. There are trade consulting meetings, high-tech products fairs, meetings for the placement of orders, lamp exhibition, food festival, and the *yangge* performance too.

The International Beer Festival in Qingdao

In mid-August, the International Beer Festival is held in Qingdao, Shandong Province.

Activities: Great singing and dancing shows, art parade, fashion shows, maritime fireworks parties, sports competition, domestic and international beer-making technology seminar, and trade consulting meetings.

Jiuhua Temple Fair

In mid-August (the lunar calendar July 30), Jiuhua Temple Fair is held in Anhui Province. There will be all kinds of Buddhist activities and ceremonies during the fair.

Watermelon Festival in Daxing, Beijing

The Watermelon Festival is held in Daxing, Beijing, from June to July. Activities: Visiting melon field, tasting watermelons, watching

folk performance, visiting peasant families.

Wine Festival of Guizhou

Wine Festival is held in Zunyi, Maotai town of the Renhuai city, Shizhang Hole of the Chishui city in Guizhou Province. Activities: Opening ceremony, visiting the culture museum, Maotai brewery, Zunyi meeting site, Shizhang Hole waterfall in Chishui, etc.

The Prairie Tourist Festival of Nadam

The Prairie Tourist Festival is held in the Inner Mongolia Autonomous Region from July 15th to August 30th. The meaning of "Nadam" in Mongolian is amusement or recreation. During the festival, activities such as Nadam fair, horse races, and palace banquet in the Yuan Dynasty style—Zama banquet, sacrificial ceremony at the Genghis Khan Tomb and wedding of Erduosi will be held.

第4章

Famous Tourist Sites in China

Beijing

Beijing, the capital of China, is the center of Chinese politics, economy, culture, transportation and travel, as well as one of the world's great historic, cultural cities and old capitals. Beijing's climate is a typical continental monsoon climate that is droughty and full of wind-blown sand in the spring, extremely hot in the summer, dry and cold in the winter and neither too cold nor too hot in the fall. Therefore, the fall is the best season for visiting Beijing, and is called the "Golden Fall of October" accordingly.

In addition to the Great Wall, splendid palaces and beautiful gardens, there are a lot of places of historic interest in Beijing: 23 sites specially protected by the state for their culture relics, 2666 existing ancient temples and 51 ashes.

Tourist Sites

Tian'anmen Square

Located in the center of Beijing's municipal area, Tian'anmen Square is the biggest square in the world—880m in length from south to north, 500m in width from east to west, and 440,000 square meters in area. The Tian'anmen Gate Tower is in the north, the Monument to the People's Heroes is in the center, the Great Hall of the People is in the east, the National Museum of China is in the west and Chairman Mao's Memorial Hall and Zhengyangmen Gate Tower are in the south.

Address: 4 Jingshanqianjie, Dongcheng District

Convenient bus routes: you can take buses No.1, 2, 4, 5, 10, 20, 52, 57, 55, 54, 120, 802 and special No.1, getting off at the Zhongshan Park stop or Tian'anmen stop or take the subway or buses No. 9, 17, 44, 48, 53, 59, 66, 110, 307, 803, 808, 819, 922, special No. 4, special No. 7,

Tuanjiehu special line getting off at the Qianmen stop.

The price for one ticket: RMB ¥ 15 (Tian'anmen Gate Tower)

The Palace Museum

The Palace Museum, named Gugong locally and also called the Forbidden City, was the imperial palace during the Ming and Qing dynasties. It occupies 720,000 square meters surrounded by high walls and a moat (also called Tongzi River) that is about 52m in width. There is a turret dotting each of the four corners of the palace. According to the layout, which is arranged symmetrically around the middle axis, the buildings can be separated into two parts, the outer palace and the inner palace. Consequently, the arrangement is clear and the main body is stressed. The emperors performed various ceremonies and hosted political activities in the outer palace, and they used the inner palace as their residence and an office to manage daily affairs.

Address: No.4, Jingshanqianjie, Dongcheng District

Zip code: 100009

Convenient bus routes: you can take buses No.1, 2, 4, 5, 10, 20, 52, 57, 22, 54, 120, 802 and special No.1, getting off at the Zhongshan Park

stop or Tian'anmen stop or take the subway or buses No. 9, 17, 44, 48, 53, 59, 66, 110, 307, 803, 808, 819, 922, special No.4, special No. 7, Tuanjiehu special line, getting off at the Gugong stop.

Tel.: 65132255

The price for one ticket: RMB ¥ 30

The price for one through-ticket: RMB ¥ 50

The Temple of Heaven

Established in 1420, the Temple of Heaven was the place where the Ming and Qing emperors worshiped heaven. It occupies 2,700,000 square meters area and is the biggest existing ancient building specifically used for making sacrifices. The Temple of Heaven is separated into an inner altar and outer altar by two layers of walls. The south walls are round and the north walls are square, representing the round sky and the square earth. Yuanqiu altar and Qigu altar are generally called the Temple of Heaven, of which the Qinian Hall is a well-known landmark of Beijing.

Address: Tiantan Road, Chongwen District

Zip code: 100050

Convenient bus routes: you can take buses No.17, 36, 64, 54, 106, 120, and get off at the Tiantan North Gate stop, or take bus No.39, and get off at the Tiantan East Gate stop, or take buses No.120, 122, 803 and special No.3, and get off at the Tiantan South Gate stop.

Tel.: 67022617, 67028866-8104

The price for one ticket: RMB ¥ 14.

Jingshan Park

Jingshan Park, part of the imperial palace of the Ming and Qing dynasties, lies at the back of the Forbidden City. The height of Jingshan's middle peak is 44.6m (its height is 88.7 meters above sea level). In the past, Jingshan's middle peak was the center of Beijing's inner city and its highest point as well. At the foot of the east slope of Jingshan, an old wrinkly pagoda tree is standing, on which Chongzhen, the last emperor of the Ming Dynasty, hanged himself when the uprising peasant army conquered Beijing.

Address: 1 Wenjin Street, Xicheng District

Zip code: 100034

Convenient bus routes: you can take bus No.5 and get off at the Jingshan West Street stop, or take buses No.58, 60 and 111, getting off at the Jingshan East Street stop, take buses No.111 and 819 and get off at the Jingshan stop, or take buses No.101, 103, 103 express, 109, 812, 814, and get off at the Gugong stop.

Tel.: 64044071

The price for one ticket: RMB ¥ 2

The Summer Palace

The Summer Palace lies in the northwest suburbs of Beijing. Established in 1750, it was the royal garden and the palace for temporary dwelling in the Qing Dynasty. The Summer Palace mainly consists of Wanshou Hill and Kunming Lake, occupying 290.8 hectares, 3/4 of which is water. Now it is no longer a royal garden but the Summer Palace, containing rich man-made landscapes and massive buildings preserved perfectly. Among the tourist attractions, the mountains and rivers, buildings, flowers and trees overlap each other, and once served the emperors in their leisure. Moreover, Foxiang Pavilion, Kunming Lake and Seventeen-holes Bridge are all very

famous scenic spots. Due to its absorption of the essence of Chinese garden art, the Summer Palace is given the title of the 'the Museum of Royal Gardens'.

Address: Yiheyuan Road, Haidian District

Convenient bus routes: you can take buses No.303, 330, 332, 333, 346, 362, 375, 801, 808, 817, getting off at the Yiheyuan stop.

Tel.: 62881144-209

The price for one ticket: RMB ¥20 (slack season), RMB ¥30 (busy season that is from Apr. 1st to Oct 31st)

The Badaling Great Wall

The Great Wall is the only man-made object which can be seen from space—China's Number One place of interest and the representative tourist attraction as well. Anyone will expect to visit the Great Wall as soon as he comes to China. By common consent, Badaling, which lies in the suburbs of northwest Beijing, is the most ideal part of the Great Wall to visit. It will take you about one hour to reach Badaling, whose height is over 1000 meters above sea level. The mountain exit of Badaling is controlled by Juyongguan Pass of the Great Wall.

Convenient bus routes: you can take buses No.969, 919 or the traveling buses of No.1, No.2, No.3, No.4 and No.5.

Tel.: 69121017

The business hours: 6:00~22:00(summer)
6:00~19:00(other times)

The price for one ticket: RMB ¥ 40 (slack season) and RMB ¥ 45 (busy season)

Address: Special Zone of Badaling, Yanqing, Beijing

Yonghe Lamasery

Located near Andingmen in northeast Beijing, this is the largest and most complete Lamasery preserved in China, except for Tibet. Every March, "an assembly praying for big wishes" with musical instruments and melodious chants is held here, "buzha" is danced and religious activities go on. Yonghe Lamasery is the treasure of Sino-Tibetan culture.

Convenient bus routes: you can take the subway (the loop line) or buses No.116, 12, 18, 44, 606, 62, 807 and special No.2.

Tel.: 64044499

The price for one ticket: RMB ¥ 25

Address: 12 Yonghegong Street

The business hour: 9:00~16:00

The Ming Tombs

This is a famous mausoleum area to the northwest of Beijing, 40km away from the city. In a small basin about 40 square kilometers in area, thirteen tombs of the emperors of the Ming Dynasty, that are called the Ming Dynasty Tombs in modern times, are distributed in an orderly fashion.

Because this area is so large, people mainly just visit two of them: the most magnificent Chang Ling and Ding Ling whose underground palace has been unearthed. Every emperor's mound has an underground palace, but only Ding Ling's has been unearthed.

Convenient bus routes: you can take bus No. 845 or traveling buses No.1, 2, 3, 4, or 5.

Tel.: 60761423

Address: Shisanling Special Zone , Changping District

Chang Ling: Opening hours: 8:30~16:30(slack-season)
8:30~17:30(busy season)

The price for one ticket: RMB ¥ 30 (slack season)
RMB ¥ 45 (busy season)

Ding Ling: Opening hours: 8:30~17:00(slack season)
8:30~17:30(busy season)

The price for one ticket: RMB ¥ 40(slack season)
RMB ¥ 60(busy season)

The Winter Palace(Yuanmingyuan)

This is located in the northwest corner of Beijing, and what we can see now is just the site of the Winter Palace. In the Qing Dynasty, it was a royal garden unparalleled in the world, which took people about 100 years from 1709 to 1809 to finish. In 1860 and in 1900, the Winter Palace was burned after being robbed by the united armies of Britain and France and the united armies of eight countries. Now, the Chinese government has turned the Winter Palace into a Site Park. You might as well visit it once you are in Beijing.

Convenient bus routes: you can take buses No.323, 365, 706, 722, 743, 951, 716, 717, special No.6, special No. 4 and the 332 branch.

Tel.: 62628501

Hutong

Once you arrive in Beijing, you should pay a visit to the *Hutongs*. There the image of old Beijing is reflected. It is said that the culture of ancient capital of Beijing is the *Hutong* culture as well as the Quadrangle culture.

If you are interested in *Hutongs*, you can take a manpowered tricycle, an ancient vehicle of Beijing, to travel pass the west side of Shicha Lake and the Yingdian Bridge, arrive at the Drum Tower and

climb the tower to see the old municipal area of Beijing and *Hutongs* extending in all directions. After that, you can go to the Houhai area to visit ancient Nanguanfang *Hutong*, Bei Guanfang *Hutong*, Dajinshi *Hutong*, Xiaojinshi *Hutong*, Qianjing *Hutong* and Houjing *Hutong*. You can enter those quadrangles and get to know the common life of local people by chatting with them. Finally, along Liuyin Street, you will get to the Gong Prince's House called "the grand garden of the red chamber," to experience the living condition and the royal garden of the old nobles.

About 100 meters away from the west side of the back gate of Beihai Park, you can find professional guides and hire a traditional tricycle to travel the *Hutongs* of Beijing.

Peking Man Site at Zhoukoudian

The Peking Man Site at Zhoukoudian is located in Longgu Hill, Zhoukoudian, Fangshan District, Beijing. It is famous for the more complete Sinanthropus fossils unearthed in the 1920s.

Address: 1 Zhoukoudian Street, Fangshan District, Beijing

Tel.: 010-69301287

Business hours: 8:30~16:30

So far, no buses go there directly. You can catch the No. 917 bus at the Tianqiao stop and change to the No.2 loop-line bus at the government of Fangshan District stop.

Shopping

Generally, the business hours of shopping centers in Beijing last from 9:30 am to 9:00 pm. As for big shopping centers and friendship stores, closing may be postponed until a later time. Especially during

Chinese holidays, shops may stay open till midnight.

The night fairs always start at dusk.

Foreign exchange and ATMs are available in bigger marketplaces and shopping malls authorized by Beijing Tourism Bureau, but you'd better have your foreign currency exchanged before you buy articles from street stalls.

No bargaining takes place when you shop in marketplaces, but if it is permitted, you should compare prices by inquiring at different marketplaces. Keep your receipts, as you may need them if you want to exchange goods. If you shop in street stalls or small shops, try to practice your bargaining skill.

In Beijing, there are a lot of big shopping centers with abundant goods such as Lufthansa, Saitec and STC. But in the top-grade marketplaces the prices will be much higher than other places. In addition, there are also some shopping streets with special features in Beijing.

Wangfujing Walking Street

Located in the north side of East Chang'an Street and next to the Beijing Hotel, Wangfujing Street has been in existance for one hundred years. On this one-kilometer street, various shops, including traditional and modern ones, are gathered. Moreover, sculptures symbolizing the traditional industry of old Beijing are placed in front of some shops. For example, the big sculptures on the walls of Tongshenghe shoe shop, an old and famous shop, and Lisheng Store are still standing, and have interested many visitors. Reconstructed specially by the Beijing Municipal Government, this street has been given the title of Number One Street in China for its unique road schemes, light design, and beautification of the road surface. However, no vehicles (with the exception of buses) are permitted to drive on this street.

Dazhalan Street

Walking around Beijing's old Dazhalan street, you can have a look at the traditional industry and business of Beijing.

The Dazhalan commercial circle located to the south of Qianmen has attracted a large number of people since ancient times. Here is the Ruifuxiang silk shop and Tongrentang Chinese traditional medicine shop, both in business for over 100 years in Beijing. Besides these there are other special stores from all over the country, such as Shanghai Lixiaoquan scissors, Tianjin *Goubuli Baozi* shop. This district is a treasure among Beijing's cultural relics.

Xiushui Street

Xiushui Street is adjacent to the American Embassy, and many diplomatic envoys come here to shop.

About 500 or 600 peddlers and businessmen gather in the outdoor fair, selling all kinds of goods such as clothes and bags, artware, silk and pearls with Chinese features. Here, there are even more foreigners than Chinese. Anyhow, foreigners and Chinese can all get what they want here, but don't forget to bargain!

Hongqiao Market

Hongqiao market lies in southern Beijing, outside the northeast wall of the Temple of Heaven.

Famous artware including cloisonné, ivory carving, jade articles and carved lacquerware are available here. What's more, all kinds of goods are offered in the second-hand jade articles district upstairs. Many of them are mimics including porcelains of past dynasties, vases from the Ming and Qing dynasties, bowlders, carnelians, emerald bracelets, old wall clocks, ancient pocket watches, snuff pots, water pipes, etc.. Hongqiao market has a good reputation among foreigners, for example, Mrs. Thatcher, the former British Prime Minister, came here to buy pearls.

Panjiayuan Antique Market

As an antique lover, you shouldn't miss the Panjiayuan Antique Market. It is said that it is the biggest artware distribution center and collection market in China. Every Saturday and Sunday, nearly thirty thousand stands gather here, attracting large number of visitors as well as overseas antique merchants to purchase goods. Here, you can find everything including porcelains from the Ming and Qing dynasties, terracotta warriors and horses, old glasses, old photos and even antique furnitures, etc.. You may feel puzzled as to how to make a choice after you walk around. The market opens during weekends and holidays only, so you may have a visit according to your time in Beijing!

Liulichang

Locating in Xuanwu District, Liulichang is a real culture street, where gentlemen and celebrities of the Qing Dynasty gathered to show their good ranks.

Liulichang is a well-arranged curio street, being divided into an east side andawestside.Inaddition tocurios, there are the "four treasures of the study" (brush pens, Chinese ink, rice papers, inkstones), traditional crafts, painting and calligraphy shops as well as stores specializing in ancient books and second-hand books. Some shops even offer overseas posting service.

Foreign Language Bookshop

Located at 235 Wangfujing Street, Dongcheng District, this shop sells hundreds and thousands of books written in 39 languages such as English, Japanese, German, French, Russian, Spanish, Portuguese,

Arabic and Serbian (including dictionaries, reference books, foreign language textbooks and reading books, foreign language reference books and domestic-edition foreign language books), audiotape and videotape products (including teaching and entertainment video tapes, laser discs, laser video discs etc.), electronic dictionaries, read-repeating and recording equipment, PC software, photograph albums, etc. Looking through the local bookshops, you may get an unexpected surprise: the book prices in China are lower than those in Europe and America.

Hotel

There are hotels of all ranks in Beijing. They are equipped with complete facilities, thoughtful service and well-trained employees, and some are under the administration of famous international groups. Luxurious rooms, shopping centers, various types of restaurants, 24-hour bars, coffee bars, international direct dial and convenient business centers are available. The price for each room conforms to international standards ranging from US$ 100 to several hundreds dollars. If you do not want to spend too much money, you can choose two-star or three-star hotels. Although they are less luxurious, they are equipped with all types of restaurants, rooms with toilets, shopping departments, post offices and small business centers too. Generally, the prices are lower than 100 dollars. Booking abroad, traveler's checks and credit cards are acceptable.

Beijing Hotel

Add:33 East Chang'an Ave.

Tel:010-65137766

Beijing Hilton Hotel

Add:1 Dongfang Rd., North Rd. of the East Sanhuan Rd.,

Tel:010-64662288

China Hotel

Add:1 Jianguomenwai Street

Tel:010-65052266

Beijing Shangrila Hotel

Add:29 Zizhuyuan Rd.

Tel:010-65128899

New Century Hotel

Add:6 Shouti South Rd.

Tel:010-68492001

Food

Roast Duck

Undoubtedly the most famous food in Beijing is roast duck. Restaurants offering roast duck are found here and there, and the tastes are also almost the same. The restaurants below are all old and famous shops:

Beijing Roast Duck Restaurant

14 West Street of Qianmen 010-63018833

Quanjude Roast Duck Restaurant

32 Qianmen Street 010-65112418

Bianyifang Roast Duck Restaurant

C-2 Chongwenmenwai Street 010-67020505

Royal Dish

As the capital of the Ming and Qing dynasties, Beijing royal or

official dishes are still available. The famous restaurants include:

Fangshan Restaurant	Inside Beihai Park	010-64011879
Tanjiacai Restaurant	7F, Beijing Hotel	
Lijiacai Restaurant	11 Yangfang Hutong	

Tianjin

Located in the northeast of the North China Plain and along Bohai Bay, Tianjin is one of the major coastal cities of China with an area of more than 11,000km^2, as well as Beijing's door to the sea. Tianjin is a well-known cultural city with a long history and one of the cradles of the Chinese Northern culture and art as well, known as the Great Wharf connecting the South and the North and "the Home of the Northern Folk Arts." The folk arts in Tianjin have gained a worldwide reputation, featuring such items as colored clay figurines by master Chang, Yangliuqing New Year Pictures, kites by master Wei, brick carvings by master Liu and especially Tianjin carpets and tapestries. Moreover, the food and catering in Tianjin are unique in China. Due to the exchange of cultures, the buildings in Tianjin have various architectural styles: Gothic and neo-classic, for example.

Tourist Sites

Food Street of South Market

Anyone visiting Tianjin should make a visit to the Tianjin Food Street to find local flavors. Here, Goubuli Baozi, Guifaxiang Large Fried Dough Twist and Golden Erduoyan Fried Rice Cake are the three unique local flavors of Tianjin, all with a more than 100 years of history. It is hard for you to pass them by without a taste.

Water Park

Located in southwestern Tianjin, the Water Park was built in 1950 with total area of 213 hectares. It is the largest comprehensive park in Tianjin, and is regarded as one of the ten major scenic spots of the city.

Every scene in the park is based on water. The water covers 100 hectares, about half of the park. In the park, there are twelve small islands between which are exquisite arched bridges with double bends, curving bridges or a causeway with willows and peaches standing along both sides. These islands divide the water into three big lakes: East Lake, West Lake and South Lake. The arrangement of trees in the park is perfect. Along the lake, the trees are mostly weeping willows; in the water, lotuses grow, and the boulevard in the island is lined with Japanese allspices, pagoda trees, chinars, etc. The water sets off the vermilion pavilions; boats, yachts, motorboats, etc. all cruise in the water. Consequently, a unique sight in Tianjin Water Park is created. However, there are some inner gardens such as Shenhu Garden, Penjing Garden, Bibo Garden, Children's Elysium, the Zoo, etc.. Especially in the zoo, you can see rare animals such as giant pandas and golden monkeys.

The Huangyuguan Great Wall

The Huangyuguan Great Wall is north of Jixian County in Tianjin, 120km away from the Tianjin municipal area and 80km from Beijing. It is magnificent in design and wonderful and graceful in shape, regarded as an outstanding part of the history of the Great Wall's construction because of its long history, various changes, smart layout and complete facilities. Here, the Great Wall Museum, Water Pass, Bagua City, Minglian Hall, etc. are unique along the whole line of the

Great Wall.

Scenic Area of Panshan Mountain

The Scenic Area of Panshan Mountain is northwest of Jixian Country of Tianjin, with a total area of 106km2. Panshan Mountain is included on the list of 15 major mountains in China, and is called "the First Mountain to the east of Beijing". As a key state-stressed scenic area, it is unique for its Five Peaks, Eight Stones and Three Windings. Now, four main areas, Rusheng, Tiancheng Temple, Wangsong Temple and Yunzhao Temple, which altogether include more than 30 scenic spots, have been opened. However, the Rusheng-Wansong Temple cableway is under use.

Wen Temple

The Wen Temple lies inside the east gate of Tianjin old town, and is also called the Confucius Temple as well. Because it stands against Wu Temple, it is commonly referred to as Wen Temple. It is the largest and best-preserved group of buildings in Tianjin. Outside the temple, there are two piety arches with two posts and three floors, built in the Ming Dynasty and rebuilt during the period of Ming's Wangli Emperor and Qing's Kangxi Emperor. They are the only remaining gate towers in Tianjin.

Dule Temple

The Dule temple is north of Xiguangkou of Jixian county of Tianjin. It was built in the Tang Dynasty and rebuilt in the Liao Dynasty, and has a combined history of over 1,000 years. Since its establishment, it has been a center for religious activities. In 1961, it was included on the list of state-stressed cultural relic sites.

The Memorial Hall of Premier Zhou Enlai and His Wife Deng Yingchao

The Memorial Hall of Premier Zhou Enlai and his wife, Deng Yingchao, is north of the beautiful Water Park of Tianjin, and occupies a total area of 6 hectares, and a construction area of 7,150m2. It is new-style cultural establishment integrates traditional culture with modern culture. The memorial hall includes the Hall to Pay Respects, Hall of Biography, Hall of Feelings as well as a video hall, multi-function hall, guest hall, research center and cultural relics house.

Shopping

Tianjin Commercial Street

Tianjin Commercial Street the Hepinglu traditional commercial street with a long history. Before the establishment of the PRC, it had developed into a market with a certain power. A lot of closely-crowed shops offer various goods and attract a large number of customers. Along this 3km long street stand the 3 famous state stores, Quanyechang Store, Hualian Shopping Plaza and Tianjing Department Store, and more than 300 medium and small shops. So, people in Tianjin prefer to call it Tianjin Commercial Street.

Binjiangdao Shopping Street

The Binjingdao Shopping Street is one of the busiest shopping streets in Tianjin. It is 2,094 meters in length total, from Zhangzhizhong Road along Haihe side to the southwest Nanjing Road.

In addition to some old and famous sites such as Quanye Store, Zhongyuan Company, Daoxiangcun Food Store, Hengdeli Clock Store, Guangming Cinema, Dengyinglou Restaurant, there are some new

marketplaces such as the Binjiang shopping plaza, Jili Mansion, International Store, and other shops. In April 1987, the market for small commodities between Shandong Road and Nanjing Road was started. At any time of day you can find people visiting here. At night, the colorful lights flash. Now, it has become a New Night Fair Sight of Tianjin.

Clothing Street

The Tianjing Garment Exhibition & Sales Center is called Clothing Street for short. It is located in Yiwei Road, Nankai district. There are more than 100 shops, retailing and wholesaling garments and textiles mostly. Famous factories and famous shops gather here to market famous-brand products, high-quality products and fashionable products. Here, you can find not only local famous and high-quality products but also famous and high-quality new products from home and abroad.

Shenyangdao Antique Market

Shenyangdao Antique Market is located at the cross of Shengyang Road, Heping District, and Shangdong Road. Now it has been developed into one of the biggest antique distributing center in China. There are some 100 shops and 300 stalls or peddlers marketing all kinds of goods including old ceramics, furniture, watches and clocks, calligraphies and paintings, 'the four treasures of the study' as well as art works made from gold, silver, copper, iron, wood and jade. Remember to bargain for a good deal.

Guyi Street

The Guyi Street is located between the northeast corner and Beidaguan, and is 800m in length.

In the past, there were only Guyi (clothing evaluation) shops on this street. Thercfore, this street was named Guyi Street. During the period of the Qing Dynasty's Guangxu Emperor, many shops selling silk and brocade, cotton cloth, fur and ceramics were also established here. Especially during the early 1930s, the business in this street reached its height, and this street became the distributing center for the North China markets for silk, cloth, fur, garments, stationery, Chinese traditional medicine and daily necessities. In addition to the peddlers everywhere, some old and famous shops such as Qianxiangyi, Ruifuxiang, Ruishengxiang, Yuanlong, Laohukaiwen, Laomaosheng, etc. gathered here.

In 1986 the street was restored and its original appearance reproduced. Large and small shops installed palace lanterns and hung signs and decorations. Some well-known traditional shops such as Ruifuxiang Silk and Brocade Shop, Qianxiangyi Baoji, Darentang Drug Store, etc. resumed their business. The buildings in the street all have antique flavors.

Hepinglu Shopping Street

The Hepinglu Shopping Street is located in the west side of Haihe River, starting from the Bohai Building in the south and ending at the southeast corner in the north. It is a modern pedestrian shopping street with famous shops, famous products and old and famous stores, and is called the Golden Street by local people. The buildings along the street combine the style of Chinese construction and Western construction, and have an ancient appearance as well as modern taste. It deserves a visit if you have the time.

Tanggu Foreign Goods Market

The Tanggu Foreign Goods market lies in Fushun Road, Tanggu

District, close to the Tianjin Development Zone, and is located in the southwest side of the crossbridge of Hebei Road of Jintang Highway. It deals with a variety of goods including automobiles, motorcycles, household electric appliances, cameras, garments, watches, lighters, acoustics etc., most of which are high-quality imported original goods sold at low prices.

Yangliuqing New Year Pictures

The Yangliuqing New Year Pictures are made of wood, and are famous among the people for their vividness, luck and impressed themes. In Chinese printing history, the Yangliuqing New Year Pictures and the famous Suzhou Taohuawu New Year Pictures were called South Peach and North Willow. They are sold in the shops in the Ancient Culture Street.

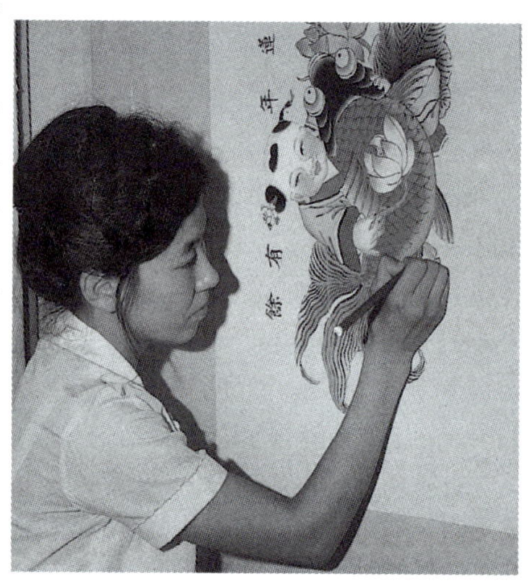

Colored Clay Figurines by Master Chang

Produced in Tianjin, the colored clay figurines are folk artwork of unique style. The founder, Zhang Mingshan, was good at making human figures. After being developed over time by his offspring, the artwork won the name of Colored Clay Figurines by Master Chang.They are sold in the shops in the Ancient Culture Street.

Hotel

Sheraton Tianjin Hotel

Add: Zijinshan Road, Hexi District

Tel: 022-23343388

Hyatt Hotel

Add: 219 Jiefang Road North

Tel: 022-23318888

The Crystal Palace Hotel

Add: 28 Youyi Road, Hexi District

Tel: 022-28356888

Astor Hotel

Add: 33 Taierzhuang Road, Heping district

Tel: 022-23311688

Tianjin Teda International Hotel

Add: 8 2nd Street, Economic Development Zone

Tel: 022-25325856

Ocean Hotel, Tianjin

Add: 5 Ocean Plaza, Hebei district

Tel: 022-24205518

Food

Food Market of South Street

The food market street is located in the South market of Heping

district. There are 34 large and medium-sized restaurants and 22 types of snack with special flavors, offering a wide variety of the major cuisines of China including Chuan, Lu, Yue, Xiang, Su, Zhe, Min and Hui as well as Jin, Jing, Islamic dishes, Western and Japanese dishes. Over 140 kinds of traditional snacks, including the three most famous traditional snacks of Tianjin Goubuli Baozi, Guifaxiang twisted sticks of dough and fried glutinous rice cakes, are also available.

Western Restaurant by German Chef

It is said that the German chef was a chef who retired from the imperialist eight Western powers during their occupation of Tianjin. After he left the army he decided to create an enterprise of his own in the oriental land since he used to be a royal imperial chef at home with excellent culinary skills. In 1901 he set up a Western restaurant in his name at the French concessions and the restaurant has remained until today. It is well known at home and abroad.

When you visit Tianjin, remember to visit this restaurant if you are free. It is located at 33 Zhejiang Road, Heping district, Tianjin.

Chongqing

Chongqing is a famous city with a long history. Clinging to mountains and near rivers, the climate in Chongqing is humid and foggy. Therefore, it has been named the Mountain City and the Fog City. As one of the most famous tourist cities in China, Chongqing offers unique Three Gorges tour resources. Because Jialing River in Chongqing was called Yu River in the past, Chongqing is also called Yu for short. Since ancient times, Chongqing has been regarded as the center of politics, military and economy of the Bayu area, as well as a key traffic position and an inland-river port on the upper reaches of the Yangtze River.

Chongqing is located in Sichuan Province, and is a well-known industrial city with the strongest science and technology in Southwest China. It was approved to be the fourth Chinese municipality directly under the control of the Central Government in 1997, becoming the only such municipality in the inland area of western China.

Tourist Sites

Dazu Grottos

The Dazu Grottos are 140 kilometers away from Chongqing. They consists of over seventy grottos, containing over ten thousand carvings in total. The two most well-known grottos are Baoding Mountain Grotto and

Beishan Mountain Grotto, which best represent the sculptural arts of the Tang (618-907) and Song (960-1279) dynasties. Most of the Dazu Grottos contain Buddhist statues and some Confucius and Taoist as well, which are the paragon of grotto arts from the later part of Chinese history. The grottos helped to boost the Chinese carving art to a higher level and played a vital role in the history of religion, art, history and culture. In the year 2000 they were listed as a world heritage site by UNESCO.

The most convenient way to get from Chongqing to Dazu is by bus. It takes a two-hour-ride to arrive. Scheduled buses to Dazu are available every day at the western bus stop of Chongqing.

The Three Gorges

The Three Gorges are composed of Qutang Gorge, Wu Gorge and Xiling Gorge.

Qutang Gorge, well known for its majesty, is on the uppermost part of the Yangtze River, starting from Baidi City in the west and ending at Daxi Town of Wushan Mountain in the east, and covering 8 kilometers in total length.

Wu Gorge is featured most for its twelve beautiful peaks, each having its own characteristics, especially the pretty and wonderful Peak of the Goddess. In addition to the twelve peaks, many other steep peaks stand out distinctly, which is described vividly in a poem.

Among the three gorges, Xiling Gorge is the longest one, starting at Zigui County in the west and ending at Yichang City in the east, covering 76 kilometers in length. It's most well known for two features: steepness and wonder.

The Smaller Three Gorges

The Smaller Three Gorges scenic area radiates from the Daning river to the suburban areas of Wushan County. The main attractions of this area are the Smaller Three Gorges of Daning River, the mini Three Gorges of Madu River, Dacheng ancient town, the cultural relic site in Daxi, and the Remains of Longgupo. Here, visitors can enjoy both the splendid views of the gorges and the ancient cultures and folk customs of this scenic area.

The most comfortable way to reach the scenic area is by boat. Every day, scheduled boats from Chaotianmen in Chongqing to Wushan Mountain are available. You can also take a bus at the Caiyuanba stop and go there directly.

Night View of Chongqing

One side of Chongqing city clings to a mountain, and the others are surrounded with rivers. The buildings on the hills and winding mountain roads provide a unique view of Chongqing, especially during the night.

As the saying goes, a visitor cannot say he has been to Chongqing without enjoying a night view of the city. Remember to climb to some high places such as the Red Star Pavilion of Pibashan Mountain Park, Kansheng Building of Eling Park, etc. to have a look at the city at night.

Fengdu Ghost City

The famous Fengdu Mount, Ghost City, is located on a hill on the Northeast of Fengdu County, Chongqing.

Fengdu Mount is a Taoist holy mountain on which stand 27 ancient temples. The Ghost City is a folk art gallery with a combination of Confucius, Taoist and Buddhist cultures.

After the completion of the Three Gorges Dam, some parts of the Ghost City will be under the Yangtze River and will become a "ghost

island".

Fengjie Town

Fengjie town, with its history of over two thousand years is located at the starting point of the Three Gorges in the west. At the mouth of Qutang Gorge, several kilometers from Fengjie town on a beautiful hill, stands the well known Baidi City—the White Emperor's Temple—a cluster of ancient red-walled and golden-roofed buildings among shaded trees, looking like a fairy land.

Fengjie town is well known as "the town of poems." Since the Tang (618-907) and Song (960-1279) dynasties, poets have written lots of poems about this town, especially the most well-known poem by Li Bai, a great poet of the Tang Dynasty, which has made this town famous all over China.

After the completion of the Three Gorges Dam, the ancient Fengjie town will be completely underwater and the Baidi City will become an island . The city walls from Yidoumen to Kaijimen will be rebuilt at Baidi Mountain. An underwater tunnel will be built connecting the new Fengjie town with the Baidi City. A new cableway will also be built between Baidi City and the Qutang Gorge.

Dacheng Old Town

Dacheng Old Town is situated in the hinterlands of the Three Gorges. It has been well known as a miniature ancient town and is the only best preserved ancient town in the Three Gorges area. The town was built in the Jin Dynasty, and has over 1,700 years of history. It has remained almost intact despite having been through many wars.

The old town has two main streets covering nearly ten hectares. The north-south street is over 150 meters long and the east-west one is over

240 meters long. There are also 37 ancient civilian brick houses with curved roofs in the style of the Ming (1368-1644) and Qing (1644-1911) dynasties and well-preserved city walls in the town. Most of the houses were built in the Ming and Qing dynasties, with grey bricks, black tiles, double eaves, curved roofs, carved beams and painted rafters, showing a simple elegance.

With the completion of the Three Gorges Dam the largest cluster of ancient architectures in the Three Gorges area will be completely under the Yangtze River. The State Culture Relics Administration is now planning to invest 30 million RMB to relocate the major residence structures of the old town.

Hotels

Chongqing Harbor Plaza Hotel

Add: Wuyi Road, Yuzhong District, Chongqing

Tel:(023)63700888

Hoi Tak Grand Hotel

Add:318 Nanpin South Road, Chongqing

Tel: (023) 62838888

West Asia Grant Hotel

Add:Xiya Plaza,33 Yuzhou Road,Chongqing

Tel:(023)68600999

Chongqing Little Swan Hotel

Add: 78 Jianxin North Road , Jiangbei District, Chongqing

Tel:(023)67870600-50105、50110

Jinli Hotel

Add: 9 Shiqiaopu Science Park Zone 2nd Road, Chongqing

Tel: (023)68626666-8560

Liyuan Grand Hotel

Add: 15 Tianchen Road, Shapingba District, Chongqing

Tel: (023)65301212;65316666

The Milky Way Grand Hotel

Add: 49 Datong Road, Yuzhong District, Chongqing

Tel: (023)63808585 Ext 1001;1002

Renmin Hotel

Add: 173 Renmin Road, Yuzhong District, Chongqing

Tel: (023)63851421

Kaixuan Grand Hotel

Add: 22 Kaixuan Road, Chongqing

Tel:(023)63806699;63809597-8105

Chongqing Guest House

Add: 235 Yuzhong District, Chongqing

Tel: (023)63845888-40674535

Marriott Chongqing Hotel

Add: 77 Qingnian Road, Yuzhong District

Tel: (023)63888888

Food

It's a great pity if you do not taste Chongqing food during your visit to the city. Chongqing food is a part of Sichuan cuisine, one of the four major cuisines in China. Sichuan cuisine is well known for its pungency and tongue numbing flavors, and is popular all over the country.

In Chongqing you can enjoy many famous Sichuan snacks. We recommend a list of them, and you can find them in any hotel in Chongqing.

Glutinous Rice Bun

This is a glutinous sesame bun stuffed with sweet fillings. It is crisp and delicious.

Glutinous Rice Cake

These are stuffed glutinous rice cakes covered with white sugar, sesame powder, sweet osmanthus and soybean flour.

Small Sweet Dumplings

The sweet dumplings with a cover of glutinous rice flour and sweet stuffing are almost transparent, and look like pearls. They are soft and delicious.

Jiuyuan Baozi

The delicious Jiuyuan dumpling bun comes with two kinds of filling. The salted ones are stuffed with pork, bamboo shoots, dry mushrooms and ham, and the sweet ones with walnuts, preserved dates, melon, orange, sugar and lard. The Jiuyuan Baozi with its thin cover and full stuffing is tasty, sweet and delicious.

Rice Flour Cake

Rice flour cakes are made from rice-flour slurry mixed with eggs, white sugar, sweet-scented osmanthus, etc. The mixture is put in a special pan and baked until it becomes golden. The cake is crisp, sweet and delicious.

Dan Dan Noodles

In the past, Dan Dan Noodles were sold by peddlers with pole on their shoulders. So they got the name Dan Dan Noodles (Dan means the shoulder pole). The noodles are a snack food with Sichuan flavor, served with dozens of condiments. The noodles are smooth and soft and the taste is delicious and spicy.

There are also many other snack foods not mentioned here. If you want to taste them, you'd better visit Chongqing yourself. It is really a pleasure to enjoy delicious food as you travel around the city.

Xiao Dongtian Restaurant

Tel：(023)63814599

Add: 107 Minquan Road, Central District, Chongqing

Zaigengxiang Restaurant

Tel: 023-62828288,62803079

Add: 52 Nanping East Road , Chongqing

Taibei Hotpot Restaurant

Tel：023-63609200

Add：Lianglukou, Central District, Chongqing

Seven Star Eel Hotpot Restaurant

Tel : 023-63727878

Add :250 Heping Road, Central District, Chongqing

Longteng Yachangwang Hotpot Restaurant

Tel: 023-65313213

Add: 197 Xiaolongkan Street, Shapingba District

Chongqing Grand Hotel

Tel: 023-65339888-6903

Add: 84 Xiaolongkan New Street, Shapingba District

Shanghai

Shanghai is located at latitude 31 degrees 13 minutes north and longitude 121 degrees 29 minutes east. Except for a few hills in the southwest, Shanghai is located on a broad plain with an average altitude of about four meters. The area of Shanghai is 6340.5 square kilometers, being about 120 kilometers in length from south to north and about 100 kilometers in width from east to west. Shanghai's climate belongs to the monsoon climate of the northern subtropics, having clearly-demarcated seasons, enough sunshine and abundant rainfall. The climate is moderate and moist, the spring and the fall are shorter than the winter and the summer and the annual average temperature is 16℃ or so. The flood seasons occur during the period from May to September including three rainy seasons: spring rain, plum rain and fall rain, when 60% of the annual rainfall falls.

Tourist Sites

St. Ignacious Cathedral

At No.158, Puxi Road, there is a famous Chinese Catholic church named Xujiahui Catholic Church, which is the cathedral of Catholicism in Shanghai parish. Its formal name is "St. Ignacious Cathedral". Next to the church, the nunnery and the office of the bishop of Shanghai parish are still standing. Xujiahui Catholic Church was built in the medieval Gothic style and can hold more than three thousand fellow believers. The sculpture of "the Virgin Mary carrying little Jesus in her arms" stands at the top of the altar, looking down the whole hall and acting as the centerpiece of the church. Tens of thousands of fellow believers in the parish will gather in the church together on Sundays and important feast days of Catholicism. Every morning, several masses are conducted. Recently, the Shanghai government designated the church as a cultural relic.

Chenghuang Temple

Located in the Fangbangzhong Road, with Anren Street to the east, Fuyou Road to the north, Jiujiaochang Road to the west, this is one of the main temples of the Zhengyi branch of Shanghai Taoism and was built at the time of Emperor Yongle (1403-1423) of the Ming Dynasty. The Chenghuang Temple was destroyed and rebuilt repeatedly throughout history, and the present Temple was built in 1926. During the Chinese Anti-Japanese War, Chinese merchants built a new Chenghuang Temple in the concessional settlement territory (which is at the crossing of Jinglingxilu of Lianyun Road and has been replaced by multi-layer residential houses). The old Temple and the Yu Garden are not only places of interest, but also ideal places for shopping, where you can find small commodities, special local products and distinctive commodities as well as big malls and famous snacks.

The Eastern Pearl Tower

Standing in Pudong Park in Lujiazui of Pudong new area, the Eastern Pearl Tower—468m high—is the highest TV tower in Asia, only shorter than Toronto TV Tower in Canada and the Moscow TV Tower in Russia.

It was constructed with the curving shape favored by oriental nationalities. The main body consists of three inclined barrels, three straight barrels and eleven spheres which form a huge space skeleton frame structure. There are six lifts in the barrels; one of the lifts is a double-decker lift that can carry 50 people, another one of them runs between the upper sphere and the capsule.

The Eastern Pearl Tower has become a landmark of Shanghai.

Yu Garden

Yu Garden is located on the south side of the Chenghuang Temple in the southern municipal area, occupying an area of more than 40 *mu* and sometimes called the City Forest for its layout characteristic of architecture during

the Wu and Yue periods. Now, it is a "culture relics protected by the state."

The wall of Yu Garden is decorated with wandering dragons and separates the garden into different scenic spots. Through the screens of false partitions, you can enjoy the garden's scenery offered in endless layers. This has become a special feature of Yu Garden. In total, there are 48 scenic spots in the garden such as the Great Rockery, Wanhua Chamber, Dianchun Hall, Huijing Chamber, Yulinglong, Deyue Chamber, the Inner Garden and others.

People's Square

The People's Square is the center of politics and culture of Shanghai, and integrates culture, forestry and beautification. It is located in the center of Shanghai. After reconstruction, its total area has now reached 140,000 squar meters.

On the middle axis of the People's Square is the City Planning Tower; in the northwest corner is the Shanghai Theater, in the northeast side is the People's Square metro station. In the south there are three underground structures, zonal HK Famous Shops Street and Dimei Shopping Center is in the southeast, toward the south lies the biggest city underground transformer substation in Asia and the biggest underground parking lot in Shanghai is in the southwest. South of the middle axis of the People's Square is the Shanghai Museum.

Shanghai Theater

Shanghai Theater lies to the northwest of People's Square with 20,000 square meters land area and 60,000 square meters construction area, containing a total of 2000 seats. A very famous French architect designed it using the most advanced material and lighting in the world, and the effect is deeply appreciated by the people of Shanghai. The structure of the Theater is a geometric shape, simple and smooth. A white arc roof like a crown extends to the sky, supporting classic outdoor theaters and air gardens, outlining the shape of a treasure bowl and representing Shanghai's absorption of the world's cultures and arts.

The Bund

The Bund is about 1500 meters in length with Baidu Bridge of Suzhou River to its north and butting Jinling East Road in the south. It has been regarded as a symbol of Shanghai for more than 100 years. In the west of the Bund, there is a group of buildings that was called "the Far Eastern Wall Street" and is now called the "National Buildings Exhibit". This group of buildings was built one after another from the 1920s to 1940s, and combines various architectural styles. Although they were neither designed by one architect nor built at the same time, they all have a similar main theme and harmonious frame line. The Bund reflects in miniature the history of Shanghai, as Shanghai reflects the semi-feudal and semi-colonial China.

Shopping

Nanjing Road

Nanjing Road starts from the Bund and extends about four kilometers towards the west, and has the reputation of being the "Number One Commercial Street in China"and also one of the busiest commercial streets in Asia. Thousands of shops stand along the street and numerous visitors gather here. Supermarkets, famous shops with 100-year-old histories, restaurants, souvenir shops and big shopping centers all do business here. Altogether there are about 360 shops in this street, selling

various types of goods such as clothes, silk, cosmetics, drugs, household appliances and many more. As a famous shopping center in Shanghai, about 500,000 visitors from home and abroad shop here each day.

Xiangyang Street

This is a small street lying to the west of Huaihaizhong Road, and also an earlier flea market in Shanghai similar to Xiushui Street in Beijing. For many years, Xiangyang Street has mainly been a market for foreign goods. The clothes, shoes and caps, bags, perfumes, glasses and accessories sold here are very fashionable, including world famous brands, though the goods are mostly made in suburban areas or Guangdong. Sometimes, the latest fashions abroad can be found here in the stalls. Many foreigners shop here, much like Xiushui Street in Beijing.

The Number One Yaohan Department Store

It is said that the Number One Yaohan Department Store in Shanghai is the biggest retail company in Asia.

Here you can not only buy things you like but also make use of banks, post offices, travel agencies, bathhouses, beauty parlors, repair houses, coffee shops and bakeries set up in each floor.

Hotels

Pacific Luck Hotel

Address: 299 Wusong Road, Hongkou District, Shanghai

Tel.: 8621-63259800

Holiday Inn Pudong Shanghai

Address: 899 Dongfang Road, Pudong District, Shanghai

Tel.: 8621-58306666

City Hotel Shanghai

Address: 5-7 Shanxinan Road, Luwan District, Shanghai

Tel.: 8621-62551133

Jin Jiang Hotel

Address: 59 Maomingnan Road, Luwan District, Shanghai

Tel.: 8621-62582582

Hilton Shanghai

Address: 250 Huashan Road, Jing'an District, Shanghai

Tel.: 8621-62480000

Pine City Hotel

Address: 777 Zhaojiabang Road, Xuhui District, Shanghai

Tel.: 8621-64433888

Huating Guesthouse Shanghai

Address: 2525 Zhongshanxi Road, Xuhui District, Shanghai

Tel.: 8621-64391818

Shanghai Jing'an Hotel

Address: 370 Huashan Road, Shanghai

Tel.: 8621-62481888

Shanghai Wanbao Hotel

Address: 660 Xinhua Road, Shanghai

Tel.: 8621-62801000

International Conference Center (Oriental Binjiang Hotel)

Address: 2727 Binjiang Ave., Shanghai

Tel.: 8621-50370000

Food

Shanghai Lübolang Restaurant

This top-grade restaurant in Shanghai was built in imitation of Ming and Qing constructions. You can gaze over the Jiuqu Bridge and the Huxin Kiosk from the second floor. The main dishes offered include local dishes, pastries, crab dinners and shark fin, which are all quite delicious though they are a bit greasier than food offered by traditional restaurants. Especially since Bill Clinton had a meal in this restaurant, it has been regarded as the first choice of tourists.

Address: 131 Yuyuan Road

Tel.: 021-63557509

Shanghai Old Restaurant

Originally named the Rongshun Restaurant, this is an old and famous restaurant with local flavor. Upon entering the restaurant, you will be surrounded by a strong atmosphere of culture. It is filled with Chinese culture and Chinese food with national characteristics, in particular local styles as well as the customs of the old city. Inside, every single decoration and furnishing has been selected and arranged specially. Customers are provided with delicious food as well as pleasant surroundings.

Address: No.242, Fuyou Road, Shanghai

Tel.:021-63111777

Xianqiangfang Restaurant

This is also a good restaurant for Shanghai food.

Address: 120 Jinxian Road

Tel.:021-62564168

Dexing Restaurant

This is a top-grade restaurant offering local food and famous Shanghai refreshments. It has been in business for about 100 years, the famous dish of which is the "Xia Zi Da Wu Shen" (shrimp roe and sea cucumber),which is reputed to be the "Number One dish in the world".

Economical snacks are provided on the first floor, a singing and dancing hall for banquets is on the second floor, and eight separate rooms and KTV are located on the third floor.

Address: 29 Dongmen Road

Tel.: 021-63743772

Xi'an

Xi'an, also known as Chang'an, is the capital of Shaanxi Province and a world-famous ancient capital. With a wealth of valuable historical sites and cultural relics, the city is called a "museum of natural history" and is an ideal place for archeology research and sightseeing.

During the Han (BC206-220AD) and Tang (618-907AD) dynasties, Xi'an was a famous international city. The well-known Silk Road started here.

The current area of Xi'an is 9,853 square kilometers and it has developed into a modern industrialized city as well as an international tourist city, with a population of 5.48 million.

Tourist Sites

Terracotta Warriors Museum

The Terracotta Warriors Museum is 1.5 kilometers away from the west side of the Mausoleum of Qinshihuang, the first Emperor

of China, and was the grave where the emperor's belongings were buried. It was discovered in 1974, and is regarded as one of the greatest archaeological achievements in the world. Pit One of the Terracotta Warriors was discovered by chance while some peasants were digging a well. Later, Pits Two and Three were discovered after drilling. Pit One is the largest, with a total area of 14,620 square meters. Over 700 terracotta warriors, 100 chariots, 400 terracotta horses and 100,000 bronze weapons were excavated from the pits. The heights of the warriors are between 1.75m and 1.85m. According to their costumes, postures and headgear, they can be categorized as officials, armored warriors and chariot warriors. Moreover, there were bronze weapons excavated such as swords, spears, halberds, tulwars, etc., which are still sharp and shining after being buried for over 2,000 years. Due to its high artistic values, the magnificent terracotta sites were included on a list of the ten greatest scenic spots in China, and designated a world culture heritage site by the UNESCO.

Mausoleum of Qinshihuang

The mausoleum is to the north of Lishan Mountain, about five kilometers from Lintong County, Shaanxi Province. It's a key cultural relic site under state protection and was listed as a world culture heritage site by the UNESCO in 1987.

The tomb is extremely large, and took 37 years to build. According to historical records, there are many hidden hazards, as well as countless rare gems and treasures, in the tomb. Though the tomb has great value, it has not yet been excavated for various reasons. We can only see a huge mound there.

Big Wild Goose Pagoda

Big Wild Goose Pagoda stands in the Temple of Great Maternal Grace in the south of the city. Master Xuan Zang was the first abbot of the Temple of Great Maternal Grace appointed by the Tang Dynasty. It was built in 652 AD for the sake of keeping Buddhist scriptures brought back by the famous monk Xuan Zang of the Tang Dynasty, after his long and arduous journey to India. He stayed, studied and translated the whole scriptures in the temple. The pagoda was also a meeting place for centuries where scholars, artists and poets showed their talents, and many of them, including the famous poets Du Fu and Bai Juyi of the Tang Dynasty, left their works behind there.

By climbing to the top of the Pagoda tourists can enjoy a panoramic view of the whole city.

Small Wild Goose Pagoda

The Small Wild Goose Pagoda is located in the Jianfu Temple, a famous Buddhist temple of the Tang Dynasty, where the monk Yi Jing spent his remaining years translating Buddhist scriptures after he had traveled to India.

The Small Wild Goose Pagoda with delicate carvings looks tall, straight and elegant. The carvings on it are fine, demonstrating the elaborate carving art in the Tang Dynasty.

More than 10 well-balanced ancient structures including pavilions, terraces, towers and halls still remain inside the yard of the Small Wild Goose Pagoda.

Drum Tower

The Drum Tower is located near the Great Mosque. It was first built during the Ming Dynasty (1368-1644) and was rebuilt twice in the Qing Dynasty (1644-1911). Originally there was a huge drum there for telling time in the dusk. The Drum Tower is 33 meters high, 52.6 meters wide, and covers 1,970 square meters.

Bell Tower

The Bell Tower stands at the center of the city. It was first built in 1384、 was relocated to the present site in 1582 during the Ming Dynasty, and was rebuilt in 1740 during the Qing Dynasty. Originally a huge bronze bell hanging beneath its roof served to tell time at dawn.

The tower sits on a square brick base, which is 8.6 meters high, 35.5 meters wide, and covers 1,370 square meters. The total height of the tower is 36 meters high.

Huaqing Pool

Huaqing Pool is located at the foot of Mt. Lishan, 35 kilometers east of Xi'an. The present pool covering 85,560 square meters was completed on the base of the pool rebuilt during the Qing Dynasty (1644-1911). In 1982 the remaining site of the Huaqing Pool of the Tang Dynasty (618-907) was found there by chance. Originally the site was the imperial bath, among which the Haitang Pool was built by Emperor Xuan Zong of the Tang Dynasty for his favorite concubine Yang Yuhuan.

Huashan Mountain

Huashan Mountain, one of the five major mountains of China, is situated in Huayin County, Shaanxi Province, 120 kilometers east of Xi'an. Neighboring Qinling Mountains to the south, Yellow River to the north, it is well known for its majestic views and perilous conditions. Huashan Mountain has five major peaks with three of them over 2,000 meters above sea level. The majesty and steepness of the mountain has attracted numerous tourists for hundreds of years.

Remains of Banpo in Xi'an city

In the eastern suburbs of Xi'an lies the ruins of what used to be a typical village of a primitive maternal commune dating from more than 6,000 years ago. It is the largest well-protected maternal village site in the Yellow River area.

The remains consist of three areas. They are living quarters, pottery kilns and graves, with the living quarters dominating. Banpo inhabitants belong to the culture of the Neolithic Age. The tools they used at the time were mainly made of stone and wood. The present museum has three relics——displaying rooms and a hall over the excavated ruins.

The Monument Forest

The Monument Forest, first built in 1090 with a history of over 900 years, is located in the compound of Shaanxi Provincial Museum.

The Monument Forest consists of seven large display halls, eight winding corridors and eight stele kiosks with a collection of more than 2, 300 steles bearing valuable inscriptions by the masters of the Chinese calligraphic art, dating from the Han Dynasty (B.C206-220A.D) to the Qing Dynasty (1644-1901). The over one thousand steles displayed here are mainly inscriptions from the Tang Dynasty. Ink stones and brushes

used by the greatest historical calligraphy masters of China are also displayed.

The City Wall of Xi'an

The city wall of Xi'an is not only the best preserved ancient urban architecture in China but also the largest and the best preserved defense system remaining in the world.

The city wall was completed in the 14th century, extending from the old wall built in the Sui and Tang dynasties during the sixth century. To be safe from attacks the wall was thickly built. It is 12 meters tall, 18 meters wide at the bottom and 15 meters wide at the top, with a total length of 13912 meters.

Since 1983, a circular park with local features has been built round the wall.

Hotels

Hyatt Regency Xi'an

Add: 158 East Street, Xi'an, Shaanxi

Tel: 029-7231234

Chang'an Grand Plaza Castle Hotel

Add: 12 Huancheng South Road, West Section, Xi'an

Tel:029-7231800

Grand New World Hotel,

Add: 48 Lianhu Road, Xi'an

Tel:029-7216868

Jianguo Hotel, Xi'an

Add: 20 Jinhua South Road, Xi'an

Tel: 029-3238888

Bell Tower Hotel

Add: 110 South Street, Xi'an

Tel: 029-7279200

Minsheng Grand Hotel

Add: 32 South Street, Xi'an

Tel: 029-7264401, 7264408

Jiefang Hotel

Add: 321 Jiefang Road, Xi'an

Tel: 029-7428946

Shopping

Antiques Street

Located near the Baxian Nunnery is a street with lots of stalls and shops specializing in antiques and arts and crafts. Local specialty articles like replicas of terracotta warriors and tri-colored glazed pottery of the Tang Dynasty, paper cuts, art fabrics and folk handcrafts are available.

Ancient Culture Street

The Ancient Culture Street lies in Shuyuanmen, Xi'an. There are dozens of shops and stalls selling books, paintings, inks and brushes and jade articles.

Xi'an Folk Art Center

Located at Xingqing Road, the Xi'an Folk Art Center specializes in tourist souvenirs, arts and crafts, the four treasures of study, silk, carpets and antique articles

Free tea and beverages are offered and international package services are also available for customer convenience. Morever, various goods are sold to meet your personal requirements. It is an ideal place for you to buy a souvenir.

Stamp Street

Stamp Street is located near Shangpu Road, Xi'an. With an area of nearly 200 square meters, it is the largest market for people to collect stamps in Xi'an. If you are interested in collecting stamps, make a visit there.

Food

Chunshengfa Pancake Restaurant

Here you can enjoy local pancakes as well as another well-known food, Hulutou, a traditional local snack with a long history dating back to the Song Dynasty (420-479A.D). This delicacy is prepared with pancakes boiled in the soup of marinated pig guts. The soup is fresh and tasty with a strong aroma.

Tel: (029)7278316, 7253693

Add: 20 Nanyuanmen, Xi'an

Snack Food Street

The food in Xi'an bears the strong characteristics of Northwest China. Tasting the snacks of Xi'an is a real pleasure. In the food street visitors can enjoy varieties of local snacks including the popular local specialty snack —mutton pancake, the world-famous "Jiaozi banquet" as well as local noodles, wheat cakes, etc.

There are several places you can savor the delicious local snacks. Beside Nanshao Gate and New East Street night markets, you can also find another snack street located just behind the Drum Tower. There are also many examples of ancient architecture for you to enjoy.

Laosunjia Restaurant

The Mutton and Beef Soup with Pancakes is a traditional specialty food of Shaanxi. The traditional food made in Laosunjia Restaurant is known for the freshness of the soup, mellowness of the meat, smoothness of the pancakes and strong tempting aromas. It also offers Islamic food, dumplings and local snacks. It is very popular with tourists both at home and abroad, and many celebrities have dined at the restaurant during the past 100 years.

Defachang

Located near the Bell Tower Square of Xi'an the Defachang was built in 1936 and consists of Defachang Jiaozi Banquet Restaurant and Defachang Hotel, both of which are time-honored brands with a high international reputation. It is a super-grade hotel of China, offering the widest variety of Jiaozi banquets in China, and also specializes in new style Shanghai cuisine.

Yunnan

Yunnan Province lies in southwestern China with a total area of 394,000 square kilometers, an average altitude of 2,000 kilometers

and a population of 40 million. It stretches over 4000 kilometers, and borders Burma, Laos, and Vietnam to the west and southwest. There are 17 counties, prefectures and cities under its administration, and Kunming is its capital.

Yunan was an important pass and port city of the ancient Silk Road in the South, with great mountains, rivers and ecologically diverse surroundings. The high mountain ranges, snow-capped all year round, are 6,740 meters above sea level and have yet to be conquered. The natural beauty of Yunnan is best represented in its ancient virgin forests, alpine landscapes, precipitous valleys, stone forests and caves formed by the karst topography.

Because of its low latitude, position on a plateau, and the influence of the sea currents, Yunnan's winter climate is dominated by the dry continent monsoon wind and in the summer is swept by humid winds from the Indian Ocean.

Due to its special landscape, Yunnan has a unique climate. A mountain might have four different seasons at four different elevations and the weather changes drastically over short distances. Yunnan has three climates within its borders—frigid, temperate and tropical—which is rarely seen in the world. Yunnan has a great number of plant and animal species due to its unique landscape and climate and the province is nicknamed 'the kingdom of animals' or 'the kingdom of plants'.

Tourist Sites

KUNMING

Xishan Forest Park

Xishan Forest Park is situated among the hills fifteen kilometers

from the western suburbs of Kunming. The main attractions in the park are the Huating Temple, Taihua Temple, Sanqing Pavilion and Dragon Gate. The Huaqing Temple is a famous Buddhist place of worship. The park blooms densely with fragrant flowers and foliage. In the park visitors can watch the sun rise up from the distant Dianchi Lake and get a good birds-eye-view of the vast lake.

The Stone Forest Scenic Area

The Stone Forest is one of the four greatest natural phenomena in China and was designated one of the first key national scenic areas in 1982. The Stone Forest, which covers 350 square kilometers, represents the most typical karst terrain landscape in the world and is called "the natural museum of sculpted landscape."

World Horticulture Expo Park

From May 1st to October 31st, 1999, the Chinese government hosted the World Horticulture Expo '99 in Kunming, Yunnan. This category A1 event lasted 184 days. The World Horticulture Expo Park

is open to tourists all year round as a key tourist attraction.

The park, located six kilometers from downtown Kunming in the Gold Hall Scenic Area, covers 218 hectares consisting of five major halls, six theme gardens, three main outdoor exhibition areas (34 domestic outdoor exhibition sections, 34 international outdoor exhibition sections and nine enterprise outdoor exhibition sections) and complete service facilities.

The park, with its enchanting surroundings of natural beauty, is a showcase of the height of the horticulture arts from China and around the world.

LIJIANG

The Old Town of Lijiang

The Lijiang old town is the main town of the Naxi minority autonomous county of Lijiang, in the northwestern part of Yunnan, 2,400 meters above sea level. The ancient town is a beautiful historic and cultural city, and is one of the few well-preserved minority towns in China.

The old town, also called Dayan town, is situated in the center of Lijiang and is China's only well-known ancient town without city walls.

The old town, well representing the Naxi culture, was listed as a national historic and cultural landmark in China and was included in the list of UNESCO's World Heritage sites.

In Lijiang you can enjoy both the beautiful natural scenery and the elegant and tranquil life of the local people. In the evening, concerts of Naxi music, entitled “the living fossil of Chinese folk music”, are held in the ancient town.

Lugu Lake

Lugu Lake is located 72 kilometers from Ninglang County, about 200 kilometers northeast of Lijiang. It is surrounded by green mountains and hills on four sides like a precious gem sitting on the plateau.

In midst of this fantastic beauty live the Mosuo people who to this day have still preserved the customs of matriarchal society. Their primitive living habits and marriage custom are unique. Men and women live separately in their mothers' homes.In a clan, the elderly women are the most respected and preside over family affairs. It's called “the Eastern matriarchal kingdom”.

Yulong Snow Mountain

Yulong Snow Mountain, located 15 kilometers from Lijiang county, is a national-level scenic area and a provincial nature reserve protection area. It has 13 peaks that are snowcapped all year round, stretching 35 kilometers from north to south, which have still not been conquered by climbers. Shanzidou, the main peak, is 5,596 meters above sea level and is the highest southernmost mountain in the Northern Hemisphere.

Yulong Snow Mountain supports rich vegetation, featuring a distinct and complete alpine vertical ecosystem going from subtropical to frigid.

Tiger Jump Gorge

Tiger Jump Gorge is flanked by the Yulong and Haba snow mountains with a height difference of 3,000 meters. The gorge is on the Jinsha River of the upper reaches of the Yangtze River and is one of the deepest gorges in the world. The gorge is 17 kilometers long with a drop of 200 meters. At the mouth of the gorge there is a huge stone sitting in the center of the narrowest spot of the river, which is only 30 meters wide. Legend said tigers often jumped off to the other side of the river there, hence the name Tiger Jump Gorge.

Many adventurous explorers tried to conquer the gorge. It's said in the 1930's, an American geographer once visited here. Up till now there are only 150 explorers who have succeeded in drifting the gorge.

DALI

Dali Old City

Dali Old City is located at the foot of Cangshan Mountain,13 kilometers from Dali City. The ancient city was first built during the Ming Dynasty (1368-1644) and was one of the first sites to be listed as a national historic and cultural city in China.

The ancient Dali city, facing the Ear Lake in the east and leaning the Cangshan Mountain in the west, has grand city walls with an original height of 7.5 meters and thickness of 6 meters, it used to have four gate towers on the four sides of the city. Clear brook water flows through the city. Simple but elegant houses in the Bai nationality style dot the landscape and in the courtyards flowers and trees flourish, looking elegant and tranquil.

In the city there is a south-north street which is lined with various shops selling local products like marble and straw articles.

Restaurants serving Bai nationality cuisine are also available.

The old town is simple and quiet.

When you visit the town you will find many hotels in the traditional style of the Bai available for your use; they are reasonably priced.

Cangshan Mountain

Cangshan Mountain, also called Diancangshan Mountain, is the main peak in the south of Yunling Mountain Range, facing Ear Lake in the east and Heihui River in the west. Cangshan has 19 peaks, with an average altitude of 3,500 meters, among which the highest is 4, 122 meters and covered with snow all year round.

Most wonderful is a brook winding between each two peaks of the mountain and flowing all year round down east to the Ear Lake. The 19 peaks and 18 rivers constitute the uniquely beautiful scenery of Cangshan Mountain.

Ear Lake

The Ear Lake (Erhai) is a famous alpine lake in Yunnan, situated at an altitude of 1,972 meters above sea level, and covering an area of 248 square kilometers. From above the lake has the shape of a new moon sitting between Cangshan and Dali Dam.

The lake water is crystal clear with little pollution and has been famous since ancient times. A visit to a Bai minority's fishing village nearby is a must since fishing villages on the high plateau are rare.

The Erhai Park in Xiaguan was built specially for tourists to better see the sights of the lake. It only takes you five yuan to get there by taxi from anywhere in the town. If you like, you can take a

tour of the lake on a boat or a yacht. Remember to bargain before agreeing to a price.

XISHUANBANNA

Wild Elephant Valley

The Wild Elephant Valley lies in the Haoyang Natural Preservation Zone, north of Jinghong City and at the place where the east forest and west forest meet. In this tropical rainforest covering nealy one million acre, a variety of plants provide wild animals such as Asian elephants and others with an ideal place to live. Herein about 300 wild Asian elephants are living. Wild elephants usually appear in groups at the riverside or in the forest and sometimes on the road. Tourists can observe their habits—searching for food, drinking, bathing, walking and playing—as well as enjoy the rainforest view there. Now the valley has been included on the list of key forest scenic areas by local and provincial administrations.

Tropical Botanical Garden

The Tropical Botanical Garden was built in 1997 and covers 80 hectares. It was actually the former Tropical Plant Institution under the Provincial Academy of Tropical Sciences. The garden is divided into thirteen themed areas, including xerophyte garden, rare plants garden, etc. The garden has a collection of over 1000 tropical plant species and has become a picturesque scenic area in Xishuangbanna.

Hotels, villas, folk art performances, fishing, souvenir shops, traditional barbecues and guide services are available for tourists in the garden.

Shopping

Dali Straw Plaited Products

Straw plaited products is the traditional art of the Bai ationality. Nearly every Bai woman has mastered the skill. There are various kinds of straw crafts such as hats, bags, boxes, mats, fans and baskets. The most popular straw articles are the hats in various styles. They are well known for their bright colors and fashionable styles.

Xishuangbanna Carpets

Using high-quality wool as the raw material, Zhaotong Carpet Plant produces traditional Xishuangbanna carpets with unique designs. The designs fully reflect the characteristics of Xishuangbanna's tropical animals and plants such as peacocks, elephants, apes, camellia flowers and other rare plants and animals. There are over 100 different designs in bright colors and fine craftsmanship.

Yunnan Baiyao

Yunnan Baiyao was first created in 1902 by Qu Huanzhang, a folk doctor from Jiangchuan County, Yunnan Province. It has a remarkable ability to stop bleeding, invigorate blood circulation, reduce inflammation. It has been widely applied in treatments of injuries. Recent research shows it also has some power to prevent cancer and tumors. The Yunfeng Baiyao developed by Yunnan Baiyao Group Co., Ltd. comes in various forms. Besides powders there are also capsules, tinctures, ointments, and aerosols.

Yunnan Tobacco

Yunnan tobacco is well known worldwide. Due to Yunnan's unique

geographic conditions, soil and climate, Yunnan tobacco features fine quality, a golden color and mellow taste, and has a good reputation among tobacco manufacturers and consumers at home and abroad. Yunnan has many popular tobacco brands such as Hongtashan, Yunyan, Yuxi, Ashima, Gonghexinxi, Hongshancha, Dachongjiu, Chahua, Shilin,etc., which occupy 70% of the market share in China.

Lunan Embroidery Works

These are the traditional arts and craft products of the Sani ethnic group. The rich patterns of different designs such as flowers, birds, fish and animals are embroidered on handkerchiefs, table cloths, dresses and shoes.

Food

Fried Corn Pancake

The snack is made of tender corn. After grinding the corn white sugar is added, then the mixture is fried with oil. Served hot it is sweet and delicious.

Crisp Baozi

Crisp Baozi are very popular in Kunming, and different from the common Baozi. The dough is kneaded with cooked lard with two kinds of stuffing (ham and sugar or fresh meat and dry mushrooms) The dumpling bun is soft and crisp with a delicious taste.

Smoked Bean Curd

This is a traditional snack in the southern part of Yunnan and is very popular in Kunming. Quality bean curd is used as the ingredient.

Fried Bee Pupae

This is made of bee pupae fried in oil. Served with salt and pepper it is nutritious with rich protein and is a specialty snack food of Yunnan.

Lunan Dairy Cake

This is produced in Shilin county of Kunming. Nutritious and tasty, this milky white snack is very popular and can be eaten raw or cooked.

Yunnan Ham Mooncake

Yunnan Ham Mooncake is made from Xuanwei brand ham and stuffed with honey, lark and white sugar. Baked with purple wheat flour, it is crisp and tasty with a strong aroma of ham. It is one of the best foods for the Mid-autumn festival and is well-known both at home and abroad.

The Eight Treasures of Yunnan

"Yunnan Eight Treasures" is a well-known snack in Yunnan. It consists of eight small cakes with different flavors in one package.

Sandao (Three–course) Tea

Originally used by King Nanzhao, Sandao Tea is a unique tea-drinking manner used by the Bai nationality in Dali to treat respected guests. It was later introduced to common folks and has lasted till the present. Sandao Tea first tastes bitter, then sweet. First, the high-quality green tea is put into a sand pot and baked over a fire. As soon as the tea becomes yellow and gives off sweet smell, some boiling water is poured over it. After the bubbles disappear it is simmered for a while. When the tea water looks amber, the first bitter tea is completed. Then the boiling water is poured into the sand pot

again, and white sugar, semen juglandis and sesame flour are added, and it is cooked again. This completes the second sweet tea. The third tea is to be made with baked cheese chips, black sugar, honey and Chinese cinnamon, completing the three-course endless flavor tea.

This old custom of Dali has developed into a public one. When drinking tea, tourists can also appreciate the folk songs and dances of the Bai people.

Qiguo Chicken

Qiguo Chicken, a famous dish of Yunnan Province, is prepared in a unique way.Two thousand years ago it was popular among the people in the south of Yunnan .It is steamed in a special steam pot named Qiguo, which keeps the chicken taste and is praised by everyone who tries it. If it is served with local herbs such as "pseudo-ginseng", "Chinese caterpillar fungus" and "rhizoma gastrodiae" the dish takes on medicinal properties besides nutritious value, and becomes an effective cure for coronary heart disease and neurasthenia.

Guoqiao Rice Noodles

Guoqiao Rice noodles are especially delicious, being composed of broth, sliced meat and seasonings. Guoqiao Rice Noodles reflect the characteristics of Yunnan dishes: abundant materials, skillful preparation and a unique style. It has won a great reputation in the world.

Hotels

KUMING

Harbor Plaza Kunming Hotel

Add: 20 Honghuaqiao

Tel: 0871-5386688

Yinghua Holiday Inn

Add: 25 Dongfeng East Road

Tel: 0871-3165888

Jinli Grand Hotel

Add: 71 North Ring Road

Tel: 0871-5153070

Jinshan Hotel

Add: North Beijing Road

Tel: 0871-5149069

Tea Garden Hotel

Add: Yongping East Road

Tel: 0871-3139208

Riyue Grand Hotel

Add: 99 East Ring Road

Tel: 0871-3312126

Taishan Hotel

Add: Xinying Small Art Road

Tel: 0871-3315991

Friendship Hotel

Add: 304 East People's Road

Tel: 0871-3328106

XISHUANGBANNA

Dai Grand Hotel

Add: 1 Minzu South Road, Jinghong City

Tel: 2125951

Traders Tea Garden Hotel

Add: Jinghong North Road, Jinghong City

Tel: 0691-2123814

Xishuangbanna Grand Hotel

Add: 1 Jinghong West Road, Jinghong City

Tel: 0691-2124249

Xishuangbanna Hotel

Add:11 Gelan Central Road, Jinghong City

Tel: 0691-2123679, Fax: 0691-2126501

Jiaotong Hotel

Add: 23 Yunjing North Road, Jinghong City

Tel: 0691-2124005

Dai Guesthouse

Add: 8 Nonglin South Road, Jinghong City

Tel: 0691-2123888

Jinghong Hotel

Add: 16 Gelan Central Road, Jinghong City

Tel: 0691-2123206

DALI

Xidian Guesthouse

Add: 11 Culture Road, Dali

Tel: 0872-2125197

Minzu Guesthouse

Add: Zhuhai Recreation Park, Dali

Tel: 0872-2124838

The No 1 Guesthouse

Add: 4 Fuxing Road, Dali

Tel: 0872-2125697

Fengcheng Hostel

Add: 2 Renmin North Road, Dali

Tel: 0872-2125565

Sports Commission Guesthouse

Add: 190 Tai'an Road, Dali

Tel: 0872-2124558

Duan Family Guesthouse

Add: Folk Custom Village, Zhoucheng, Dali

Tel: 0872-2451017

Post Commission Guesthouse

Add: 4 Jianshe East Road, Dali

Tel: 0872-2123708

Taxation Commission Guesthouse

Add: 7 Fuxing Road, Dali

Tel: 0872-2125409

Weishan Guesthouse

Add: 33 Dongxin Road, Wenhua Town, Weishan County, Dali

Tel: 0872-6122655

LIJIANG

Senhe Grand Hotel

Add: Gucheng New Road, Lijiang

Tel: 0888-5120891, 5120892

Xiaoliangshan Hotel

Add: Lingyuan Road, Ninglang Town

Tel: 0888-5521246, 5521247

Lugu Hotel

Add: Opposite Xingzhonglu Plaza, Ninglang Town

Tel: 0888-5522862, 5524221

Mosuo Resort

Add: Red Rock Development Zone, Lugu Lake West

Tel: 0888-5881179

Yunhang Tourist Hotel

Add: Snow Mountain Central Road, Lijiang

Tel:0888-5160188

Tianshengqiao Spring Resort

Add: Tianshengqiao, Chongdian County, Diqing Prefecture

Tel:13708822724

Yuquan Hotel

Add: Hongtaiyang Plaza North, Dayan, Lijiang

Fax:0888-5123926

Red Camellia Grand Hotel

Add: Ring Road, Dayan Town, Lijiang

Tel:0888-5125588

Lijiang Lite Hotel

Add: Snow Mountain Central Road, Lijiang

Tel:0888-5166999

Kaitian Hotel

Add: Dayan Town, Lijiang

Tel:0888-5187999

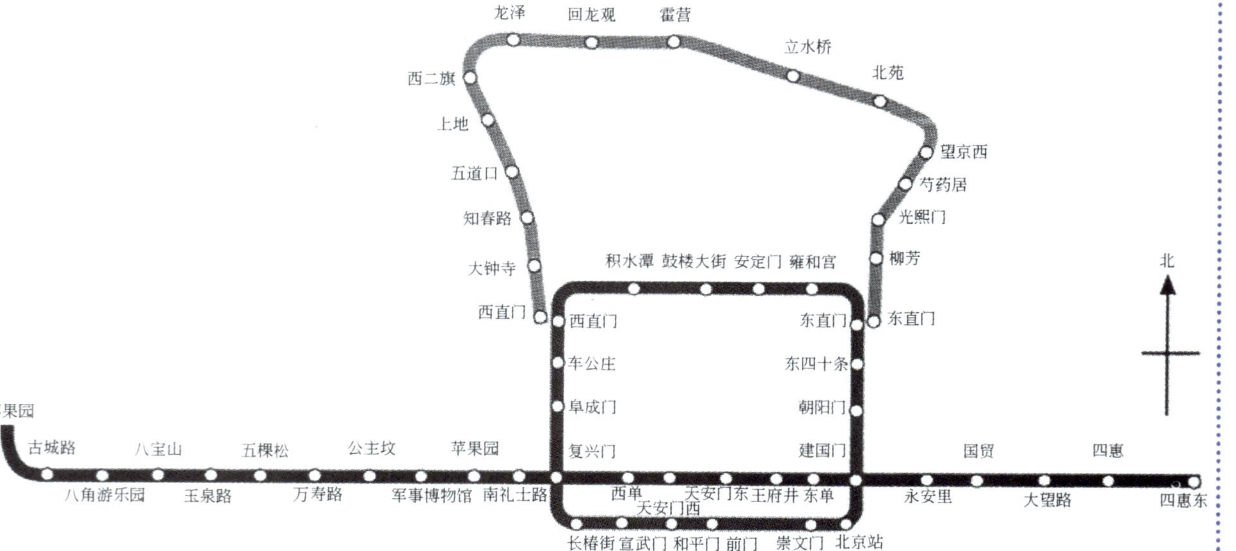

北京市地铁、城铁示意图

A Map of Beijing Metro System

中文编辑：曲　径
英文编辑：韩　晖
封面设计：何永妍
印刷监制：佟汉冬

图书在版编目（CIP）数据

学汉语　游中国 / 耿京如编著；曲径改编.- 北京：华语教学出版社，2003.10
ISBN 7-80052-926-6
Ⅰ.学… Ⅱ.①耿…②曲… Ⅲ.旅游 - 汉语 - 口语 - 对外汉语教学 - 教材　Ⅳ.H195.4
中国版本图书馆 CIP 数据核字（2003）第 087593 号
韩国时事出版社授权华语教学出版社在中国独家出版发行汉英版

学汉语　游中国

作　者：耿京如　夫　伯
改　编：曲　径
*

华语教学出版社出版
（中国北京百万庄路 24 号）
邮政编码　100037
电　话　：(86)10-68995871
传真：(86)10-68326333
网址：www.sinolingua.com.cn
电子信箱：hyjx@sinolingua.com.cn
北京市松源印刷有限公司印刷
中国国际图书贸易总公司海外发行
（中国北京车公庄西路 35 号）
北京邮政信箱第 399 号　邮政编码　100044
新华书店国内发行
2005 年（大 32 开）第一版
（汉英）
著作权合同登记图字 01-2002-5414
ISBN7-80052-926-6/H·1511(外)
9-CE-3682P
定　　价 36.00 元